Front cover | Umschlagvorderseite | Couverture
The Cymbalista Synagogue and Jewish Heritage Center, Tel Aviv, Israel

Back cover | Umschlagrückseite | Dos de couverture
Sketch for chapel, Monte Tamaro, Ticino, Switzerland

Page 1 | Seite 1
Mario Botta, 1999

Page 2 | Seite 2
Single Family House, Daro-Bellinzona

Acknowledgement | Danksagung | Remerciements
The publisher and author wish to thank Paola Pellandini from Studio
Mario Botta for her kind assistance in the preparation of this book.

Der Verlag und der Autor danken Paola Pellandini vom Studio
Mario Botta für ihre freundliche Unterstützung bei der Entstehung
dieses Buchs.

L'éditeur et l'auteur tiennent à remercier Paola Pellandini du Studio
Mario Botta pour son aimable soutien lors de la réalisation de ce livre.

Edited by Caroline Keller, Cologne
Co-edited by Christiane Wagner, Stuttgart
Design: Catinka Keul, Cologne
Cover Design: Catinka Keul, Cologne
French translation: Jacques Bosser, Paris
German translation: Annette Wiethüchter, Berlin

Printed in Italy
ISBN 3–8228–2344–9

Mario

Botta

Philip Jodidio

KÖLN LONDON LOS ANGELES MADRID PARIS TOKYO

Contents | Inhalt | Sommaire

Stone, Light, and Reason

The road to Mogno, in the Maggia Valley, winds through some of the most beautiful scenery in southern Switzerland. Born of centuries of tradition, the rough-hewn stone architecture of this area is singular. The Maggia River is one of the prime sources of alpine water for Lake Maggiore, and the stones from the riverbed and local quarries are well known for their quality. Despite, or perhaps because of, its jagged cliffs and spectacular waterfalls, the Valle Maggia is a bucolic haven in summer, an isolated world unto itself. Near the uppermost reaches of the valley sits the tiny village of Mogno, which seems far removed from any conceivable violence. Yet an ominous high mound, today covered with grass, extends toward the town from the towering mountains above. This is the most visible trace of a catastrophic double avalanche that destroyed Mogno on April 25, 1986. Near the base of the mound, the Church of Saint John the Baptist was recently completed, replacing the seventeenth century edifice that stood on the same site until that fateful night.

It is a measure of the significance of this place that Rudolf Arnheim, Professor emeritus of Harvard University and the noted specialist of the psychology of art, has chosen to write the following words on the symbolism of architecture: "All works of art worth their name are symbolic, and works of architecture are no exception. By symbolism, I mean that these works, in addition to their physical functions, such as that of sheltering, protecting and facilitating the activities of their users convey through their visible appearance the spiritual and philosophical meaning of their functions ... This symbolic meaning is not simply an attribution applied to the building by some thinker 'from the outside' as a kind of added interpretation, but it is of the very nature and essence of the design itself. ...

"In designing a new church [for Mogno], Mario Botta avoided the paralyzing effects of the closed symbols of traditional church architecture. His church is modern in style, shockingly different, but in no way struggling for sensational novelty. On the contrary, it aspires to meet the demands of a temple of worship by deriving them simply and directly from expressive traits of basic geometrical shapes. Botta's church reaches for the sky and meets Leon Battista Alberti's demand that it be 'isolated from, and raised above, the surrounding everyday life.'"[1]

This description of the symbolism of the church in Mogno goes directly to the heart of the work of Mario Botta, who was born in Mendrisio in the Canton of Ticino in 1943. As Botta says, "I am a native of Italian Switzerland, but from the cultural point of view I feel more Italian than Swiss. The culture of Italy has nourished me: you might even say that it is in my chromosomes. Thus my architectural knowledge is in many ways ecclesiastical. The history of architecture that I know is that of churches from the Romanesque to Ronchamp. When you think about it, you realize that Mediterranean culture is very much one of churches. Ninety percent of what we know and retain of the Romanesque, of the Renaissance or of the Baroque is related to religious buildings. Of course, the modern period is more one of civil construction, but one always has hidden debts."[2]

The Language of Stones

Clad in alternating bands of white Peccia marble and gray Riveo granite, the church in Mogno is indeed based on geometric shapes – circle, ellipse or truncated cylinder, – forms that led to long debate among the more traditionally minded residents of the area. And yet within, it is hardly the cold geometry of Modernism that comes to mind. An eighteenth century wooden crucifix hangs above an arched opening behind a wooden altar designed by Botta. The heavy stone and gray/white pattern here bring to mind

Tamaro Chapel

1 Arnheim, Rudolf: "Notes on religious architecture," in: *Languages of Design – Formalisms for Word, Image and Sound.* Volume 1, No 3, August 1993, Elsevier Publishers, Amsterdam.
2 Interview with Mario Botta, Lugano, August 16, 1998.

the very debts that Mario Botta speaks of. As much as it is contemporary, the church in Mogno is also anchored in the distant past. "I firmly believe," says Botta, "that my roots, my love for this profession, come from the architecture of the Middle Ages, from the Romanesque, and perhaps also from vernacular architecture. The durability of the architecture one sees in the Valle Maggia is exemplary. It is beyond style or fashion, even beyond local culture. It is archetypal."[3]

Church of Saint John the Baptist, Mogno

The church in Mogno is not the only one designed by Mario Botta. Another chapel stands on a mountain peak closer to Lugano. The debate over the architect's project for the Valle Maggia was intense in the Canton of Ticino in the late 1980s. Though some came to his defense, many felt that his design was inappropriate for this mountain village. One of those who favored Botta was Egidio Cattaneo, the owner of a ski lift located near the highway linking Lugano to Bellinzona. Here, at an altitude of ca. 2,000 meters, near the Monte Tamaro, he asked the architect to build a chapel in memory of his late wife. With its uninterrupted view over the valley of Lugano, this is one of the most spectacular works of contemporary European architecture. Its rugged power is defined not only by its strong forms, but also by its unusual cladding of rusticated porphyry. The whole is completed by a group of frescoes by the Italian painter Enzo Cucchi, who seems to have been very much in tune with the spiritual nature of the architect's scheme. Both the chapel itself and its decor are indisputably modern, and yet they also appear to spring from much older forms.

When asked if he is a religious man, Botta replies, "I have what I would call a layman's concept of religion. I truly believe that architecture can create emotions. It can give us a desire for spiritual values, such as silence. Silence is the language of stones. Silence is very rare in the modern world, and yet it can still be found in concert halls and churches. I love churches because they make you feel that you are the protagonist. You are more than a shadow. In fact, you must be able to enter a church and feel that you are at the center of the world. I believe that this idea of the sacred corresponds to a primordial need of man. What is sacred is apart from the rest, and the founding gesture of architecture is to trace a limit, to create a space. Its interior must necessarily be different from its exterior; thus the concept of the sacred is implicit in the very origins of architecture. Creating architecture is a sacred act because it separates one condition from another. Mies van der Rohe reduced this issue to a few centimeters of glass. I love the old architecture that remains capable of resisting, of affronting the outside world with its own means, not those of electricity or a curtain of warm air."[4]

Whether it be out of love for the past, or because of his conviction that interior and exterior must be distinct, it is clear that Mario Botta gives great importance to the walls of his buildings. They are massive and heavy, cast in concrete or clad in brick. They mark a tactile boundary, a limit, which as he says, "separates one condition from another." In this respect he sets himself apart from much contemporary architecture, which seeks to confuse interior and exterior, or to downplay the significance of the wall. Mario Botta's work is almost diametrically opposite to the architecture outlined in a recent Museum of Modern Art show in New York called "Light Construction," which highlighted the efforts of such designers as Kazuo Sejima or Herzog & de Meuron. Although he is necessarily pragmatic about the art of construction, admitting that an architect must adapt himself to the conditions of a given project, the very massiveness of his walls emphasizes the fact that his style has been remarkably consistent since the beginning of his career. In a period, as he says, of ephemeral architecture, this very fact may lead some to condemn Mario Botta as being out of touch with the times.

Despite his avowed interest in Romanesque or vernacular architecture, and his desire to return to certain fundamental values (see following pages), Mario Botta is deeply indebted to the

3 Ibid.
4 Ibid.

Single Family House, Riva San Vitale

Modern Movement. He makes the point that the founders of Modernism had in mind many of the values that he defends today. "Architecture," he says, "is the art of organizing space. This is so obvious that it seems to have been forgotten. In a culture of consumption and of the ephemeral, what remains is only a caricature of architecture. By returning to essential values, I believe that we can contribute to the advancement of modernity, as Le Corbusier, Alvar Aalto or Louis Kahn imagined it. Their response to industrial society was to think in terms of the basic needs of men. Despite the criticism that his work draws today, Corbu was one of the rare men of this century to have understood such basics as the seasons or the solar cycle. These are the only things that remain. The rest disappears like burning cardboard. The heritage of the modern that interests me is the question of the ethics of the built environment, the need to respond forcefully to current needs."[5]

Even those of little religious conviction must feel that the Santa Maria degli Angeli chapel on the Monte Tamaro (1990–1996) is an exceptional place. Like a long, narrow parapet at the edge of the world, it leads the visitor to a small platform where he is indeed the protagonist, almost to the exclusion of any other visitor. Hanging above this spectacular valley, or below, within the chapel itself, where the enormous hands painted by Enzo Cucchi behind the altar wait to gather up the faithful, doubters may be given pause. This is the womb, or the sacred heart, the center of all things. With its unusual arched form and rough cladding, the chapel on that mountain is like a witness from times forgotten or times to come to the deep currents that run through any man or woman. What some would call spirituality, others might call humanity. Both are present in this place. In Mogno and on the Monte Tamaro, Mario Botta has created evocative structures, which certainly look back to the architecture of the past for a part of their inspiration. Although they are places of worship, these buildings seem to be imbued with a spirituality that is not specifically Catholic, perhaps because they have not adopted shapes that are typically associated with churches. This may be due to what Botta refers to as his "layman's concept of religion," but it also touches on the central issue of the function of architecture.

On this subject, Mario Botta's comments are enlightening: "I am more and more convinced, that the architect works in the territory of memory. I believe that many of the functional aspects are in fact ephemeral. My work on churches has helped me to return to the essential values of architecture, which are gravity, light, materials, and forms, structured in order to create a dialogue. Building a church like that of Mogno today is an act of resistance against the culture of the ephemeral. Everything that is not essential must be eliminated. This is an attitude that I find that I share with a number of contemporary architects, such as Tadao Ando or, in a different style, Alvaro Siza. This is more a question of ethics than it is one of aesthetics."[6]

The Wall and the Circle

Mario Botta's reputation as an architect was based at first on his spectacular private houses, which very often stand apart from their environment. Powerful geometric compositions, they sometimes evoke fortifications. His single family house in Riva San Vitale (1971–1973) is a tower approached from the rear by a red metal bridge. More recently, his house in Daro-Bellinzona (1989–1992) is driven like a wedge into a hillside, again bringing to mind the idea of a defensive architecture. He contests such a "military" interpretation of his work, preferring a more physiological one.

5 Ibid.
6 Ibid.

"The house," he says, "is intimately related to the idea of the shelter. A cave carved out of the rock is like a mother's womb. This is the concept of the house that I defend. When I am tired of the world, I want to go home. There I can regain my energy to prepare for the next day's battle. As long as there is a man who needs a house, architecture will still exist. The house I built in Morbio, for example, is partially dug into the mountain – it is a cavern that opens out onto the sky. The cavern and the sky. Defensive architecture," he concludes, "is meant for physical combat. A house should be like a mother's womb."[7]

Whether it is in his private houses, or in larger structures, the preferred vocabulary of Mario Botta is geometric – round, square or rectangular, – but necessarily geometric. Curiously, when describing his concept of the house, Mario Botta draws a free form, more evocative of the womb than of his own buildings. When asked why he is so insistent on a reduced vocabulary of shapes, he responds energetically: "I am tolerant enough to say that I even like the work of Alvar Aalto! What I defend is the idea that architecture must be distinct from nature. Primary forms, geometry, help me to underline the difference that exists between the reason and poetry of the built world and nature. The concept of 'organic architecture' confused everything. If there is no more nature, there can be no more culture. The castles and bell towers of the past were clearly works of man. The monumentality and the geometry that I seek are based on that simple observation. In my mind this is not a question of style, but one of the very language of architecture."[8]

From his point of departure in the Canton of Ticino, Mario Botta has gone forward to earn an international reputation, more recently based on large buildings such as the San Francisco Museum of Modern Art or the Evry Cathedral. Although stylistic elements such as his geometric vocabulary or use of brick in cladding remain, buildings on a much larger scale pose different problems, particularly when they are set in an urban context. It may be asked, for example, whether the somewhat closed nature of his buildings really permits them to participate in the continuity of urban life. Naturally, he refutes this criticism.

Located on Third Street in downtown San Francisco, the Museum of Modern Art (1989–1995) is a large structure, measuring 60 x 83 meters and rising to a height of 44 meters. It is clad in prefabricated concrete panels with a brick veneer facing. Mario Botta declares that: "In a contemporary city, the museum is elevated to the status of a new cathedral, a place for the memory of and relationship with other epochs, as filtered through the works of art exhibited. But it is also an urban focus. Today as never before, its role is of great significance in an urban context constructed less and less by design and more and more by conglomeration." And yet the closed nature of the façades, together with the building's unusual monumentality, may give it an almost funerary aspect. "The façades are very closed," says Botta, "because we didn't need façades. On the contrary, what I sought was the idea of a wall, with a single slit in the middle. I gave the priority to the interiors, where windows were of little use. If you put windows in a museum, curators tend to shut them. I am of course not the first to have discovered this. In Schinkel's museums, walls have great importance."[9]

As for the funerary interpretation, Mario Botta retorts, "Today, people don't really grasp the significance of ancient monuments. Since their original message is not understood, they have been emptied of their substance. I would maintain that in this instance we are quite distant from funerary architecture. The city of the dead is full of symbolism and nostalgia. What wasn't accomplished in life is carried out there."[10] It is implicit that the architect feels that there is none of the "symbolism and nostalgia" of funerary architecture in his museum design.

Watari-um Contemporary
Art Gallery

7 Ibid.
8 Ibid.
9 Ibid.
10 Ibid.

There was no competition as such held for the choice of the architect of this centrally located 20,900 square meter museum. Rather, the Trustees of the San Francisco Museum of Modern Art, which was created in 1935, interviewed six architects: Mario Botta, Frank Gehry, Thomas Beeby, Tadao Ando, Arata Isozaki and Charles Moore. Located near the Moscone Convention Center, the museum, which opened on January 18, 1995, is part of an urban redevelopment program covering an area of more than 40 hectares, first envisaged by the city of San Francisco in 1954. Built on city land put at the disposition of SFMOMA by the redevelopment agency responsible for the Yerba Buena district, the new structure was erected at a cost of $60 million, provided almost entirely by private donations. A central *oculus* that appears on the exterior of the building in the form of a truncated cylinder brings light to the five stories of the building, and particularly to the generous, seven-meter high top-lit galleries on the upper floor.

The SFMOMA is located across the street from Fumihiko Maki's Yerba Buena Center, whose light, ship-like style seems at odds with Botta's massive, windowless structure. Indeed, these buildings by two of the best-known contemporary international architects have very little in common. Since Mario Botta insists greatly on the importance of urban values, this lack of dialogue might seem surprising. "I don't want to criticize a colleague," says Mario Botta, "but what Fumihiko Maki built is a sort of open pavilion in a garden. Although his building is located on a corner, it opens instead onto a park. Suffice it to say that a European architect would have designed this as a corner building. Two different visions of urban design are on display here. I consider that my building is much more urban, even if it is closed. The word 'closed' doesn't mean anything in this instance. The Museum, with its monumental doorway, faces the street."[11] In a similar vein, Mario Botta criticizes James Stewart Polshek for having placed the high, blank wall behind the stage of his theater on the Third Street side, instead of making an entrance there. "For me," concludes Mario Botta, "in architecture, the wall, even a blank one, must have a certain transparency. I can see what is behind a wall – a theater, an art gallery or an empty space. A wall, when it is properly designed, can be far more evocative of what is within than glass, which I find to be the most fundamentally opaque construction material."[12]

The museum designed by Mario Botta for the work of the artist Jean Tinguely in Basel (1993–1996) also includes a number of closed façades. Although this structure is not as large as the San Francisco Museum of Modern Art, it is placed in a very dense urban environment, dominated here on one side by a major highway. Another side of the Museum faces the Rhine, and this is precisely where Mario Botta has chosen to add an unusual element. The "barca" is a long, curved glass walkway that hangs from the building, offering visitors a view of the Rhine before they enter the exhibition areas. "When I designed the museum," says Botta, "I wanted the visitors to realize that they were only a few meters from the Rhine. This is why I designed this 'obligatory' entrance. It is a sort of aperitif, an introduction to the museum, that is intended to create a dialogue between the visitor and the city."[13] The blankest façade of the Tinguely Museum faces the elevated highway, isolating visitors from its noise and distracting sights. In this instance, Mario Botta also makes a gesture to local architecture by cladding his building not in his trademark brick, but rather in red sandstone, which was also used for the minster of Basel.

Museum Jean Tinguely

11 Ibid.
12 Ibid.
13 Ibid.

Paradise and Hell

As the most important religious edifice built in France for over a century, the Evry Cathedral (1988–1995) was bound to come under close scrutiny. Many criticized the Catholic Church for spending 60 million French francs at a time when many people are in need, but the project was funded entirely with donations. The Cathedral attempts to give a center to an unattractive *ville nouvelle* that was created without any real sense of urban design. Located just to the south of Paris, Evry does gain a measure of coherence thanks to Botta's design, despite the unusual shape of the Cathedral.

Calling on the truncated cylindrical form that he often favors, Botta erected this 4,800 square meter church with a reinforced concrete structure, and brick cladding on both the exterior and interior. It was built with no fewer than 800,000 bricks made in Toulouse. The interior benches, which seat 800 persons at ground level, and 400–500 more in upper galleries, are made of Burgundy oak, and, like the white Carrara marble altar and baptismal font, were designed by the architect. The apparently unusual 38.5 meter circular plan in fact makes reference to Byzantine churches (for example to the Church of the Holy Sepulchre in Jerusalem), and in this respect looks back to the origins of Christianity. An unusual triangular metal frame carries the roof structure, admitting generous amounts of daylight and making the interior very agreeable, if not as obviously spiritual as in Ando's chapels, for example.

For some, with its circle of trees around the upper level, the Cathedral of Evry brings to mind the head of Christ with the Crown of Thorns. "I honestly never thought about it," responds Mario Botta to this idea. "The cylinder has no façade. By cutting off the cylinder at an angle, I wanted to transform the roof into a kind of façade. I never thought of the Crown of Thorns because I do not believe in direct symbolism. A symbolic transposition in architecture can very easily become a caricature. In an entirely mineral environment, creating a kind of garden on this public building is ideal. I wanted to add an element that would move with the wind. In fact I had a similar notion in the case of the San Francisco Museum of Modern Art where I originally proposed a number of mobile structures for the roof, something like works by Calder."

It is worth pursuing the reasoning that led Botta to the circular form in Evry, because it holds a key to understanding his architecture. Even if the trees on the Cathedral are not intended to be evocative of the Crown of Thorns, the circular shape of the building could be interpreted in the light of Botta's own idea of the house as shelter. Since the church is intended as the "house of God," might not its round, truncated shape symbolize the ultimate shelter – that of the human skull? "Any interpretation is possible," says the architect, "but for me the round form is the most essential one. It is the shape that offers a maximum floor surface with a minimum area of façade. It is a powerful, difficult form that has only one center. Like a solar clock, it receives the light of the sun in a different way every day of the year. Whether you see it from the exterior, or from the interior, you immediately understand a round building. As Heidegger said, a man inhabits a space as soon as he is able to orient himself. If you cannot orient yourself, you are in a labyrinth, and it is my feeling that all of modern culture, with few exceptions, is headed in that direction. In any ordinary shopping center, you have to have directions to orient yourself!" And here, Mario Botta gives a more profound explanation of his own attachment to geometric shapes, related still to the idea that one must be able to orient oneself. "Permitting you to know where you are is a great quality of a built space," he says. "Geometry does not resolve every problem, but it can permit the architect to avoid falling into the abyss of the labyrinth. The labyrinth is hell. Orientation is paradise!"[14]

14 Ibid.

San Francisco Museum of Modern Art

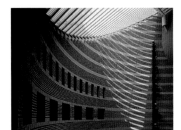
Evry Cathedral

The work of Mario Botta is, in almost every instance, recognizable. Through his choice, both of materials and of forms he has created one of the clearest "signature" styles in contemporary architecture. He readily admits that his often-categorical statements are subject to the numerous influences that play on any building project. "Granted," he says, "everything I do cannot be dictated by the strictest interpretation of my ideas, but even pragmatic decisions can allow for a certain continuity. The language of my architecture is inside of me. Picasso used the same language to create two very different works, the 'Demoiselles d'Avignon', and 'Guernica'. The same signs can be used to create a declaration of love or an ethical statement that men should not kill each other. I can recognize the style of Gabriel García Márquez, or the symbols of a Paul Klee that speak to the child within every one of us. Giacometti often asked why he kept sculpting the 'same' head, why he couldn't do exactly what he wanted. I can recognize the style of Tadao Ando," concludes Mario Botta. "We have similar preoccupations even if we use a different language. He uses concrete, but we have the same concern about light and materials."

The Urban Conundrum

The issue of urban design is a frequent one in the work of Mario Botta. Whether in San Francisco, in Basel, or in the small town of Evry, he attempts to take into account the built environment, and to "reinforce" its fabric, as he says. It can be said that his commitment to powerful urban statements finds a relatively easy territory in neat, orderly Swiss cities such as Lugano or Basel. Even San Francisco, in the midst of the Yerba Buena district, is strictly orthogonal, and well suited to the alignment that the architect found in the Third Street entrance. Can such certainty coexist with a more complex or chaotic urban area? Mario Botta maintains that it can, and cites as an example his Watari-um Contemporary Art Gallery in Tokyo (1985–1990). Set on a very small triangular lot (157 square meters) in the midst of a city known for its extremely chaotic urban patterns, the Gallery retains Botta's characteristically powerful walls and geometric design.

The text of a letter written by Mario Botta to his client describes his point of view about this building: "I was born in a tiny country village located between Milan and the Alps to the north. Even as a child, when the imaginary was still real, within my hamlet I dreamed about the immensity of great, distant cities. Today, I still love to pursue those highly intense sensations and feelings that helped me during those years of my childhood. Tokyo heightens the contradictions of the 'modern' city. The dimensional and spatial contrast with the preexisting context is physically perceptible on every street corner. Alongside the wounds inflicted by new developments a dense urban context survives; its pre-industrial matrix preserves memories of spatial relationships that now stand in direct contrast to the new architecture. In the Babel of urban languages that changes daily, I wanted to test the 'durability' of a strong, primary image, an architecture generated by the building's own inner logic, its geometry and the effects of light. My hope is, dear 'difficult' Mrs. Watari, that 'our' Watari-um will live for centuries, like the Romanesque buildings."[15]

For those who know Tokyo well, Mario Botta's wish that his building will "live for centuries" might seem a bit pretentious. Here is a city that has been destroyed twice in this century, by earthquake, fire and bombs. Here is a city that changes on an almost daily basis, remaking itself constantly, a place

[15] Letter to Mrs. Watari, August 5, 1990.

where the ephemeral rules, despite the historic layering of urban patterns that underlies the whole. To hope that 157 square meters in the heart of the metropolis would be spared such a fate is more an act of faith in the solidity of architectural design and construction than it is a reasonable assessment of what the future may hold. It might even be called an act of hubris, were it not for the ironic tone employed by the architect, vis-à-vis his "difficult" client. Yet, in this respect, Mario Botta is of course not alone. The great architects of our time often have a justifiably high opinion of themselves.

San Francisco Museum of Modern Art

But then, Botta turns his analysis of the Watari-um Gallery in an unexpected direction. As he says, he wanted to "test the 'durability' of a strong, primary" form in a chaotic city. "Accepting chaos is harder than you think," continues the architect. "You would have to be very strong to do that. The Swiss sculptor Jean Tinguely was able to transform a kind of chaos into poetry, but he was an exceptional artist." Here, the architect returns to a more seemly modesty that nonetheless emphasizes the ways in which he wishes to be set apart from other architects. Many contemporary Japanese architects, for example, have espoused the idea that a city like Tokyo in fact represents a higher level of human organization than orthogonal Western cities. Their thought, in part based on mathematical "chaos theory," may have some foundation, and it does lead them to very different aesthetic decisions than Mario Botta.

The theories underlying the work of Mario Botta, as he expresses them, are indisputable insofar as his reference to the "basic values" of architecture is concerned. An awareness of materials, light, and the ability of a visitor to orient himself hardly can be contested in any building, whether ancient or modern. When Mario Botta speaks of the vernacular architecture of the Valle Maggia, he evokes the idea of archetypal designs. By going back to the past and attempting to seek out fundamental values without ever lapsing into a "post-modern" pastiche, he is, as he points out, also returning to the very bases of the Modern Movement.

"What I defend," says Mario Botta, "is the idea that architecture must be distinct from nature." His powerful geometric forms and massive walls also often tend to set his buildings apart from others, even in an urban environment. Like his early house in Riva San Vitale, his work can seem somewhat aloof or even isolated. Like a "maternal womb," his houses are intended to shelter and to clearly delineate interior and exterior. Since he finds that much of contemporary architecture, fascinated by the labyrinth and the ephemeral, is to be rejected, it may be quite natural that his work is often distinct not only from nature, but also from its built environment. Mario Botta does place great emphasis on "reinforcing" the urban fabric when he works in a city. There is a substantial effort on his part to seek alignments or to complete existing compositions, as he does for example in his Office Building "Ransila 1" in Lugano (1981–1985), or his upcoming Museum of Modern and Contemporary Art (and Cultural Center) in Rovereto (Trento), Italy (1993–). But it may be that not every visitor to the San Francisco Museum of Modern Art, for example, finds brick walls to be quite as transparent as the architect does.

The Golden Section

The best understanding of the importance of Mario Botta's work may still be found where this text began, in the beautiful mountain scenery of the Maggia Valley. Set among mostly rebuilt houses in the village, the church (1986/92–1998) stands out as a symbol. Though it has nothing of the appearance of a traditional church, it reaches upward in a way no other type of edifice could. Manifestly circular, it also verges toward the ellipse, and these shapes have their significance, as Rudolf Arnheim points out. "It is a simple stone cylinder, quite different from the shape to which the villagers had been accustomed. Not that starkly simple shapes are alien to rural living – one is reminded of the silos on our own farms – but to be presented with such a cylinder as the local church must be startling. More precisely, the cylinder of the building is elliptical in section, and somewhere above the height of the human body it begins to be cut off by an oblique plane. This harsh interruption of a perfect shape might remind villagers of the ruins, several of which they saw after the avalanche struck. ... Since the roof is covered with glass, it orients the building and its congregation to the sun, as churches have traditionally done. Moreover, the tilted plane of the roof is given by the architect the shape of a perfect circle.

"The building as a whole plays on the symbolically evocative interplay of ellipse and circle. Panofsky, in his essay on Galileo as a critic of the arts, has reminded us that Galileo refused to adopt his friend Kepler's discovery that our planetary system does not consist of a set of concentric circles, but of elliptical trajectories with the sun placed in one of the foci of these ellipses. The perfect symmetry of the Copernican system was in keeping with the Humanistic belief that the perfection of God was best expressed in the perfect geometrical shape of the sphere or circle and that therefore the appropriate shape of the sanctuary was centric and circular."[16]

Aside from the reference to the theories of Galileo and of Kepler, Mario Botta's frequent use of the circular form is indicative of the nature of his quest for fundamental values. A basic shape that exists in nature as well as in art, the circle has extensive ramifications in the psychology of visual perception as well as in the very foundations of architecture. *Enso*, the circles drawn by Zen Buddhist monks in a single stroke, symbolize emptiness, oneness, and the moment of enlightenment. Nor is this mystical significance totally unrelated to the power of the church in Mogno, for example.

Rudolf Arnheim defines in his book *Art and Visual Perception*, first published in 1954, the importance of the circle as the most fundamental shape: "It has been maintained that the child receives the inspiration for his earliest shapes from various round objects observed in the environment. The Freudian psychologist derives them from the mother's breasts, the Jungian from the *mandala*; others point to the sun and the moon. These speculations are based on the conviction that every form quality of pictures must somehow be derived from observations in the physical world. Actually the fundamental tendency toward simplest shape in motor and visual behavior is quite sufficient to explain the priority of circular shapes. The circle is the simplest shape available in the pictorial medium because it is centrically symmetrical in all directions."[17] This last point clearly recalls Botta's own explanation: "For me the round form is the most essential one."

Recalling that Ernest Rutherford first represented the structure of the atom as a series of concentric circles in 1915, the French art historian and philosopher René Huyghe points out that men have on occasion imposed their own preconceived notions of geometry on natural phenomena, as did Galileo.[18] And yet circles, in particular concentric ones, do frequently exist in nature. Huyghe cites the waves that radiate from any point of impact as an obvious example. In 1767, in his *History of Electricity*, the English theologian and scientist Joseph Priestley sought to explain the rings (known as Priestley's rings) that are formed by an electrical discharge on a metallic surface. So too, Sir Isaac Newton noted the circular patterns of light diffraction. It can be observed in passing that Botta's

Office Building "Ransila 1"

16 Arnheim, Rudolf: "Notes on religious architecture," op. cit.
17 Arnheim, Rudolf: Art and Visual Perception. A Psychology of the Creative Eye, University of California Press, Berkeley, California, 1974.
18 Huyghe, René: *Formes et forces, de l'atome à Rembrandt*. Flammarion, Paris, 1971.

chapel in Mogno has an elliptical ground plan, and an apse with concentric bands of white marble and gray granite. The point here is that the circle is more than a modernist, geometric shape. It is a fundamental element of the languages of nature and of human perception.

In architecture, the significance of the circle is far-reaching. In his work on the Golden Section, Matila C. Ghyka points to the significance of the circular form as described by Vitruvius in deriving the basic north-south axis that was essential to the orientation of ancient architecture.[19] From there, the subdivision of the circle by inscription of a pentagon, or a decagon for example, was the basis of the proportions of much ancient architecture, from Egyptian temples to Rome and even through the design of Gothic churches and of Renaissance buildings. The basic, round form of such well-known buildings as the Pantheon in Rome (118–128 A.D.) or Donato Bramante's "Tempietto" (1502) serves to highlight the circular, often centrally planned, shape that reappears throughout the history of architecture. The ellipse is present as well in such structures as Bernini's S. Andrea al Quirinale (1658–1670).

Superimposed on the geometry of the circle, a great variety of symbolic meanings emerged as each civilization, each period, added its own interpretation. In the East, *mandala*, *stupa* or *enso* assume this most basic form, while the halo graces the sacred personages of many times and places. One of the most visually arresting and significant artistic representations of the circle might be Leonardo da Vinci's study of the proportions of the human body (1485–1490), his "Vitruvian" man. The "perfection" of man is here expressed as a relation to the circle. The omnipresence of the circle in the attempt to derive the ideal proportions of architecture from those of the human body can also be seen in the Vitruvian figures of Cesare Cesariano, or Francesco di Giorgio. Closer to our time, and undoubtedly more significant for Mario Botta, drawings for the *Modulor* of Le Corbusier, based on the Golden Section, also depict the human body inscribed in two circles. In many of the drawings used to present his projects, Botta takes up the *Modulor* figure of Corbu to give an idea of the proportions of the spaces.

In his book *The Dynamics of Architectural Form*, Arnheim writes: "Man can use the forms of architecture to declare himself a rational creature generating rational shapes. As such he feels antagonistic to nature's appearance and perhaps superior to it. He may even undertake to make nature itself conform to this ideal of rationality." This analysis certainly brings to mind the "crown" on the Evry Cathedral or the lone tree perched at the highest point of the "Ransila 1" building in Lugano. "While in the gardens of his own making," pursues Rudolf Arnheim, "man imposes his order on the irrationality of nature, he can also point up an order underlying nature's disorderly appearance. If all natural things consist ultimately of the five regular stereometric solids, as Plato maintained in the *Timaeus*, or if the multifarious variety of natural appearance is derived from the complex application of simple laws, then this inherent lawfulness can perhaps be evoked in nature by the presence of the pure geometrical shapes that only man can conceive and build. Thus a tower on a hill creates an accent around which nature may organize itself in a comprehensible order."[20]

This stereometric tower in a natural setting could well resemble Botta's house in Riva San Vitale. "What I defend is the idea that architecture must be distinct from nature," says Mario Botta. "Primary forms, geometry, help me to underline the difference that exists between the reason and poetry of the built world and nature." And yet the very basic form of the circle, frequently present in his work, is very much a part of the natural world, and has profound meanings in the history of art, philosophy and religion. The circle, which Mario Botta naturally does not employ in every building he designs, may be seen here as a symbol of his

19 C. Ghyka, Matila: *Le nombre d'or*. Gallimard, Paris, 1982.
20 Arnheim, Rudolf: *The Dynamics of Architectural Form*. University of California Press, Berkeley, California, 1977.

Tent for the 700th Anniversary of the Swiss Confederation

thought. Substantively linked to the very roots of architectural history, symbolic in many faiths of "emptiness, oneness, and the moment of enlightenment," the circle is also a primary, geometrical figure that few could suspect in any sense of being a pastiche.

And here the link between past and present becomes apparent. The fundamental simplicity sought out by the founders of Modernism was often very much in harmony with the great architecture of the past. The *tabula rasa* declared by Gropius did little to clarify this issue, but Mario Botta is not so much seeking to prove his modernist credentials as he is looking for the *values* that presided over the creation of the great buildings of the past. In Greece, Rome, Renaissance Italy, or at Ronchamp (Notre-Dame-du-Haut), these are often values of humanism. Even where a stronger force may be evoked, as on the Monte Tamaro or in Mogno, there is first and foremost an understanding of human experience, inscribed in an eternal circle, sheltered by strong walls.

In recent times, few have sought with such consistent effect as Mario Botta to bring contemporary architecture back to its roots. Nor are these roots the superficial ones that inspired pastiche façades in the post-Modern years. Rather these are the roots that go back to the origins of the built environment, and that do pass through the strong founders of the Modern Movement. Light, orientation, and a determination to make architecture stand apart from the natural world, are elements common to the great structures of many civilizations throughout the ages. Granted, other times and places may have found nature on the contrary to be an inspiration. Gothic architecture calls on the imagery of the tree, while the Romanesque that Botta admires is more firmly anchored in primary forms. The very massiveness of Mario Botta's walls, echoing back to a time when buildings were meant to stand for centuries, places him apart in a time of "light construction."

He feels an affinity for the Japanese architect Tadao Ando, who may have gone even further in paring buildings down to their essential concrete, geometric minimum. Ando too favors thick walls that sharply delineate interior from exterior. He too constructs a shelter, particularly when he builds a house. Like Ando, Botta seems more successful when he builds small, powerful buildings than when he attempts to apply similar principles on a larger scale.

Mario Botta is a man from a mountainous country whose intellectual heritage places him even more firmly than geography south of the Alps. Though he occasionally uses steel and glass in visible quantities, Botta is a man of stone, of brick, and of concrete. Even when he built a tent for the celebration of the 700th anniversary of the Swiss Confederation (1989–1991) he seemed to want more to refer to the ancient traditions of nomadic peoples than to make any concession to the ephemeral world of today. Shaped like a cupola and topped by the 26 flags of the cantons, it took its place in the Castelgrande of Bellinzona as though it was part of an archaic design. To say that Mario Botta's work is modern and yet firmly anchored in the past is to say that he has succeeded in his quest as an architect.

Cymbalista Synagogue

Stein, Licht und Rationalität

Church of Saint John the
Baptist, Mogno

Die Straße nach Mogno im Maggia-Tal windet sich durch eine der schönsten Landschaften im Südosten der Schweiz. Traditionell aus grob behauenem Naturstein errichtete Bauten haben hier Jahrhunderte überdauert. Der Fluß Maggia sammelt als einer der Hauptzuströme für den Lago Maggiore die Wasser der Alpenbäche, und seine Flußsteine sowie die Steine aus den Steinbrüchen der Gegend sind für ihre gute Qualität bekannt. Trotz – oder vielleicht eher wegen – seiner schroffen Felsen und beeindruckenden Wasserfälle ist das Valle Maggia im Sommer ein ländlich-idyllischer Zufluchtsort, eine abgeschiedene kleine Welt für sich. Am oberen Ende des Tals befindet sich das Bergdorf Mogno, über dem eine vollkommen ungestörte Ruhe zu liegen scheint. Doch erstreckt sich ein merkwürdig hoher, mit Gras bewachsener Hügel von den hoch aufragenden Bergen bis in das Dorf hinein. Er ist die sichtbare Hinterlassenschaft einer gewaltigen zweifachen Steinlawine, die Mogno am 25. April 1986 überrollte und zerstörte. Am Fuß dieser Erhebung ist vor kurzem die Johannes dem Täufer geweihte Kirche fertiggestellt worden und ersetzt nunmehr das Kirchengebäude aus dem 17. Jahrhundert, das an gleicher Stelle bis zu jener schicksalhaften Nacht gestanden hatte.

Rudolf Arnheim verweist auf eben diesen Ort, um die Symbolkraft der Architektur und die Bedeutung von Mogno in diesem Zusammenhang herauszustellen: »Alle Kunstwerke, die diesen Namen verdienen, sind symbolisch, und Architekturwerke bilden darin keine Ausnahme. Mit Symbolismus meine ich, daß diese Werke zusätzlich zu ihrer physisch-materiellen Funktion – Zuflucht zu bieten, zu schützen, ihren Nutzern bestimmte Aktivitäten zu ermöglichen – uns durch ihr äußeres Erscheinungsbild die spirituelle und philosophische Bedeutung ihrer Funktionen vermitteln ... Diese symbolische Bedeutung ist nicht einfach ein Attribut, das irgendein Denker dem Gebäude ›von außen‹ aufoktroyiert – als eine Art weitere Interpretation –, sondern gehört zur Natur und zum innersten Wesen des architektonischen Entwurfs. ...

Bei seinem Entwurf der neuen Kirche [für Mogno] vermied Mario Botta die lähmende Wirkung der geschlossenen Symbole traditioneller Kirchenarchitektur. Seine Kirche ist modern, gewagt und völlig anders, wobei sie in keiner Weise sensationell neu sein will. Im Gegenteil, sie strebt danach, die Funktionen eines Gottesdienstraums zu erfüllen, indem sie diese einfach und direkt aus ausdrucksvollen geometrischen Grundkörpern ableitet. Bottas Kirche streckt sich in den Himmel und erfüllt Leon Battista Albertis Forderung, eine Kirche solle sich ›vom umgebenden Alltag isolieren und sich darüber erheben‹.«[1]

Diese Erläuterung der Symbolik der Dorfkirche von Mogno trifft zugleich das Wesen von Mario Bottas Œuvre. Botta wurde 1943 in Mendrisio im Kanton Tessin, Schweiz, geboren und sagt von sich selbst: »Ich bin ein gebürtiger Italienisch-Schweizer. Was die Kultur angeht, so empfinde ich mich selbst jedoch eher als Italiener denn als Schweizer. Die Kultur Italiens hat mich genährt ... man könnte fast sagen, sie steckt in meinen Chromosomen. Deshalb sind meine Architekturkenntnisse in vielerlei Hinsicht die der Kirchenarchitektur. Die Architekturgeschichte, die ich kenne, dreht sich um Sakralbauten – von den romanischen Kirchen bis zu Ronchamp. Bei genauerer Betrachtung erkennt man, daß die mediterrane Kultur weitgehend eine kirchlich geprägte Kultur ist. Neunzig Prozent dessen, was wir über romanische, Renaissance- oder Barockgebäude wissen, bezieht sich auf Sakralarchitektur. Natürlich geht es in der Moderne mehr um bürgerliche, zivile Bauten, aber man hat ja immer verborgene Schulden.«[2]

Die Sprache der Steine

Mit ihrer Fassade aus im Wechsel angelegten weißen Peccia-Marmor- und grauen Riveo-Granit-Bändern ist die Kirche von Mogno tatsächlich auf der Basis geometrischer Formen entstanden:

1 Arnheim, Rudolf: »Notes on religious architecture«, in: Languages of
Design – Formalisms for Word, Image and Sound, Bd. 1, Nr. 3,
August 1993, Elsevier Publishers, Amsterdam.
2 Gespräch des Verfassers mit Mario Botta in Lugano, 16. August 1998.

Kreis, Ellipse und Stumpfkegel – Elemente, die von den eher traditionell denkenden Bewohnern der Gegend kontrovers diskutiert wurden. Und dennoch tritt im Innern der Dorfkirche kaum die kühle Geometrie der modernen Architektur vor Augen. Ein Holzkruzifix aus dem 18. Jahrhundert ist über einem Bogenfenster hinter dem Holzaltar angebracht, den Botta entworfen hat. Die massiven Steinmauern und ihr grau-weißes Muster lassen an genau die »Schulden« denken, die Botta angesprochen hat: Die Kirche in Mogno ist zwar sehr modern, offenbart aber gleichzeitig ihre Wurzeln in der Vergangenheit. »Ich bin fest davon überzeugt«, so Botta, »daß meine Wurzeln, meine Liebe zu diesem Beruf, in der Architektur des Mittelalters liegen, in der Romanik und vielleicht auch in der volkstümlichen Architektur. Die Dauerhaftigkeit der Bauten, die im Valle Maggia zu sehen sind, ist beispielhaft. Sie liegt jenseits von Stilen oder Moden, sogar jenseits der Lokalkultur. Sie ist archetypisch.«[3]

Nicht nur in Mogno findet sich ein Sakralbau Mario Bottas. Ein weiteres Kirchengebäude erhebt sich auf einer Bergkuppe in der Nähe von Lugano. Die Debatte um den Entwurf des Architekten für die Kirche Johannes des Täufers im Valle Maggia wurde Ende der achtziger Jahre im Kanton Tessin mit großer Intensität geführt. Obwohl sich einige Stimmen zu Bottas Verteidigung äußerten, empfand doch die überwiegende Zahl der Kritiker das Konzept als unpassend für dieses kleine Bergdorf. Einer von Bottas Befürwortern war Egidio Cattaneo, Inhaber der Seilbahn, die sich nahe der Autobahn von Lugano nach Bellinzona befindet und zum Monte Tamaro hochführt. Cattaneo beauftragte den Architekten, hier, auf einer Höhe von ca. 2 000 m ü.d.M., eine Kapelle zum Gedenken an seine verstorbene Frau zu errichten. Die Kirche, die in dieser exponierten Lage einen freien Blick über das Tal von Lugano ermöglicht, ist den eindrucksvollsten Werken der zeitgenössischen europäischen Architektur zuzurechnen. Ihre rohe Kraft ergibt sich nicht nur aus ihren massiven Formen, sondern auch aus ihrer ungewöhnlichen Fassadenverkleidung aus Porphyr-Bossenquadern. Kongenial zur spirituellen Qualität des architektonischen Entwurfs führte der italienische Maler Enzo Cucchi die Fresken aus. Die bauliche Gestalt wie auch die künstlerische Ausstattung sind unbestreitbar modern und scheinen dennoch archaischen Formen zu entspringen.

Auf die Frage, ob er religiös sei, antwortet Botta: »Ich habe das, was man ein laienhaftes Verständnis von Religion nennen könnte. Ich glaube wirklich, daß Architektur Emotionen erzeugen kann. Sie kann den Wunsch nach spirituellen Werten in uns wecken, zum Beispiel nach Schweigen und Stille. Die Stille ist die Sprache der Steine. Stille und Schweigen sind in unserer modernen Welt sehr selten, man findet aber beides noch in Konzertsälen und Kirchen. Ich liebe Kirchen, weil sie einem das Gefühl geben, ein Hauptdarsteller zu sein. Man ist mehr als ein Schatten. Tatsächlich sollte man in der Lage sein, eine Kirche zu betreten und das Gefühl zu haben, im Mittelpunkt der Welt zu sein. Ich glaube, daß diese Konzeption des Heiligen einem Grundbedürfnis des Menschen entspricht. Alles Heilige ist von allem übrigen abgesondert, und die grundlegendste Geste der Architektur ist das Errichten einer Begrenzung, die Schaffung von Raum. Das Innere muß sich notwendigerweise vom Äußeren unterscheiden, und deshalb gehört die Vorstellung vom Heiligen wesentlich zu den Ursprüngen von Architektur. Bauen ist eine heilige Handlung, weil sie den einen Zustand vom anderen trennt. Mies van der Rohe reduzierte dieses Thema auf ein paar Zentimeter Glas. Ich liebe die alte Architektur, die fähig bleibt, der Außenwelt mit ihren eigenen Mitteln zu widerstehen, zu trotzen. Und diese Mittel heißen weder Elektrizität noch Warmluftschleier.«[4]

Ob aus Liebe zur »alten Architektur« oder aus der Überzeugung heraus, daß Innen- und Außenraum differenzierbar bleiben sollten – Mario Botta mißt den Außenmauern seiner Gebäude

Tamaro Chapel

3 Ibid.
4 Ibid.

große Bedeutung zu. Sie sind sichtlich massiv, in Beton gegossen oder mit Ziegelmauerwerk verkleidet, und markieren eine greifbare Begrenzung, eine Grenze, die – wie Botta sagt – »eine Situation von der anderen trennt«. In dieser Hinsicht distanziert er sich von einem Großteil der Gegenwartsarchitektur, die die Trennung von Innen- und Außenraum aufzulösen sucht oder zumindest die Bedeutung der Umfassungsmauer herabsetzt. Mario Bottas Baukunst ist das genaue Gegenteil der kürzlich in einer Ausstellung des Museum of Modern Art in New York unter dem Titel »Light Construction« – Leichtbauweise – umrissenen Architektur; präsentiert wurden vor allem Werke von Kazuo Sejima, Herzog & de Meuron und Gleichgesinnten. Obwohl Botta notwendigerweise pragmatisch an die Kunst des Bauens herangeht und anerkennt, daß ein Architekt seinen Stil der jeweiligen Aufgabe anpassen sollte, unterstreichen doch gerade die massiven Mauern seiner Bauten die Tatsache, daß er selbst vom Beginn seiner Karriere an bis heute in stilistischer Hinsicht bemerkenswert beständig geblieben ist. In einer Periode der »ephemeren Architektur«, so äußert Botta, mag diese Tatsache einige Kritiker zu dem Vorwurf veranlassen, er habe den Kontakt zur heutigen Zeit verloren.

Trotz seines erklärten Interesses für romanische und »volkstümliche« Architektur und trotz seines Bestrebens, wieder auf gewisse Grundwerte zurückzukommen (auf die im folgenden näher eingegangen wird), ist sich Mario Botta des Einflusses der klassischen Moderne bewußt. Er weist darauf hin, daß deren Initiatoren viele der Qualitäten befürworteten, für die er selbst heute eintritt. »Architektur ist die Kunst der Raumgliederung«, sagt er. »Das ist so offensichtlich, daß es offenbar vergessen worden ist. In einer Kultur des Konsums und der Flüchtigkeiten bleibt nur noch die Karikatur von Baukunst. Indem wir zu wesentlichen Werten zurückkehren, können wir – glaube ich – zur Förderung der Moderne beitragen, so wie es sich Le Corbusier, Alvar Aalto oder Louis Kahn vorgestellt haben. Sie reagierten auf die Industriegesellschaft, indem sie die Grundbedürfnisse des Menschen erfüllen wollten und entsprechend planten. Trotz aller Kritik, die heute an Le Corbusiers Bauten geübt wird, war er doch einer der wenigen Architekten dieses Jahrhunderts, die so grundlegende Gegebenheiten wie die Jahreszeiten oder den Sonnenlauf verstanden. Das sind die bleibenden Fakten. Alles andere vergeht wieder wie Papier im Feuer. Das Erbe der Moderne, für das ich mich interessiere, ist die Frage der Ethik, die unserer gebauten Umwelt zugrunde liegt, und die Notwendigkeit, kraftvolle Lösungen für aktuelle Bedarfsfälle zu entwickeln.«5

Selbst Menschen mit geringer religiöser Überzeugung empfinden die besondere Ausstrahlung, die von der Kapelle Santa Maria degli Angeli (1990–1996) auf dem Monte Tamaro ausgeht. Dies ist der Mittelpunkt aller Dinge. Mit ihrer ungewöhnlichen Bogenform und Fassade aus roh behauenen Porphyrsteinen wirkt die Kapelle am Monte Tamaro wie ein Zeugnis aus uralten oder auch aus kommenden Zeiten. Einige mögen es Spiritualität nennen, andere Menschlichkeit: Beides ist an diesem Ort lebendig.

Hier und in Mogno hat Mario Botta evokative Formen geschaffen, die sicherlich zum Teil von der Architektur der Vergangenheit inspiriert sind. Obwohl es sich um Bauten handelt, die speziell für Gebet und Gottesdienst errichtet wurden, scheinen sie erfüllt von einer Spiritualität, die nicht explizit im katholischen Glauben wurzelt. Dies mag zu tun haben mit dem, was Botta als seine »laienhafte Auffassung von Religion« bezeichnet.

Das Phänomen berührt aber gleichzeitig die zentrale Frage nach der Funktion von Architektur. Mario Bottas Ausführungen zu diesem Thema sind sehr aufschlußreich: »Ich bin mehr und mehr davon überzeugt«, sagt er, »daß der Architekt auf dem Feld der Erinnerung arbeitet. Ich glaube, daß viele funktionelle Aspekte der Architektur tatsächlich flüchtiger Natur sind. Meine Arbeit an Kirchen hat mir geholfen, zu

Housing, Monte Carasso

5 Ibid.

den wesentlichen Werten der Baukunst zurückzukehren, als da sind: Schwerkraft, Licht, Materialien und Formen – alle so strukturiert, daß sie einen Dialog schaffen. Eine Kirche wie Mogno zu bauen ist heute ein Akt des
Widerstands gegen die Kultur der Flüchtigkeit. Alles Unwesentliche muß entfernt werden. Diese Haltung teile
ich mit einer Reihe meiner Zeitgenossen, zum Beispiel mit Tadao Ando oder, in einem anderen Stil, Alvaro Siza.
Es ist gleichermaßen eine Frage der Ethik wie der Ästhetik.«6

Singe Family House, Daro-
Bellinzona

Mauer und Kreis

Sein Ansehen als Architekt begründete Mario Botta zunächst durch eine Reihe
von Einfamilienhäusern, die sich von ihrer jeweiligen Umgebung deutlich abheben. Es sind ausdrucksstarke
geometrische Kompositionen; gelegentlich erinnern sie an Festungen. Sein Einfamilienhaus in Riva San Vitale
(1971–1973) ist ein quaderförmiges Turmhaus, das auf der Rückseite über eine rote Metallbrücke erreichbar ist.
Das Haus in Daro (Bellinzona) (1989–1992) ist wie ein Keil in einen Hang hineingetrieben – beide Gebäude
lassen an eine Architektur der Verteidigung denken. Botta jedoch widersetzt sich einer derartigen »militäri-
schen« Interpretation seines Werks und zieht eine physiologischere Erklärung vor.

»Das Haus«, so sagt er, »ist eng verbunden mit der Vorstellung von einer Schutz-
hütte. Eine in den Felsen gehauene Höhle ist wie ein bergender Mutterleib. Das ist das Entwurfskonzept des
Wohngebäudes, das ich vertrete. Wenn ich müde bin von der großen weiten Welt, möchte ich nach Hause
gehen. Dort kann ich neue Energien tanken, um mich auf die Mühen des nächsten Tages vorzubereiten. Solan-
ge es noch einen Menschen gibt, der ein Haus braucht, wird es auch Architektur geben. Das Wohnhaus, das ich
in Morbio Superiore gebaut habe, ist zum Beispiel zum Teil in den Berg eingegraben. Es ist eine Höhle, die sich
zum Himmel öffnet. Die Höhle und der Himmel. Zweck der Verteidigungsarchitektur ist der Kampf. Ein Haus
sollte dagegen wie ein Mutterleib sein.«7

Ob Einfamilienhäuser oder größere Gebäude – Bottas bevorzugte Formensprache
greift auf die elementaren geometrischen Körper zurück: Kreis, Kugel, Würfel oder Zylinder. Es fällt allerdings
auf, daß Bottas Skizze, die er zur Erläuterung des Konzepts für sein eigenes Haus zeichnet, eher mit dem viel-
zitierten Mutterschoß, das heißt der Gebärmutter, in Beziehung zu setzen ist als mit seiner Architektur. Auf die
Frage, aus welchem Grund er auf einem reduzierten Formenvokabular bestehe, antwortet er mit Nachdruck:
»Ich bin so tolerant zu sagen, daß mir sogar die Bauten Alvar Aaltos gefallen! Ich trete lediglich für die Vorstel-
lung ein, daß Architektur sich von Natur unterscheiden sollte. Primärformen, das heißt geometrische Formen,
helfen mir, den Unterschied zwischen der Rationalität und Poesie der gebauten Umwelt einerseits und der
Natur andererseits zu unterstreichen ... Wenn es keine Natur mehr gibt, kann es auch keine Kultur mehr geben.
Die Burgen und Glockentürme alter Zeiten waren ganz offensichtlich Menschenwerk. Die Monumentalität und
Geometrie, die ich anstrebe, basieren auf dieser simplen Beobachtung. Für mich ist das keine Frage des Stils,
sondern eine Frage der ureigensten Sprache der Architektur.«8

Von seinem Tessiner Büro aus hat sich Mario Botta international einen Namen
gemacht, in jüngerer Zeit vor allem aufgrund seiner Großbauten wie dem San Francisco Museum of Modern
Art oder der Kathedrale von Evry. Obwohl er bestimmte Stilelemente – gewisse geometrische Formen oder
Ziegelfassaden – beibehält, stellen sich beim Bauen im größeren Maßstab andere Probleme, besonders wenn
es sich im städtischen Kontext vollzieht. Es wäre zum Beispiel kritisch zu fragen, ob der eher »verschlossene«
Charakter seinen Gebäuden wirklich gestattet, zur »Kontinuität« im städtischen Leben beizutragen. Botta
indes weist diese Kritik zurück.

6 Ibid.
7 Ibid.
8 Ibid.

Das Museum of Modern Art (1989–1995) an der Third Street in Downtown San Francisco ist ein Bau von gewaltigen Ausmaßen: Im Grundriß mißt er 60 x 83 m und erhebt sich bis zu einer Höhe von 44 m. Die Fassadenverkleidung besteht aus vorgefertigten, mit Ziegelsteinen verblendeten Betonplatten. Mario Botta hat dazu bemerkt, daß »das Museum in der zeitgenössischen Stadt in den Status einer neuen Kathedrale erhoben wird; zu einem Ort der Erinnerung an andere Epochen, an dem man einen Bezug zur Geschichte findet, wie sie sich durch den Filter der hier gezeigten Kunstwerke darstellt. Es ist aber auch ein städtischer Brennpunkt. Wie nie zuvor hat es eine wichtige Funktion in einem städtischen Kontext, der immer weniger das Ergebnis gezielter Stadtplanungen, sondern vielmehr das Resultat planloser Zusammenballungen ist.« Die Hermetik der Fassaden verleihen dem Museumsbau jedoch im Verbund mit seiner Monumentalität nahezu den Charakter eines Mausoleums. »Die Fassaden sind deshalb fast ganz geschlossen«, so Botta, »weil wir keine Fenster brauchten. Ich wollte die Idee von einer Mauer mit einem einzigen Schlitz in der Mitte verwirklichen. So konzentrierte ich mich insbesondere auf die Innenräume, in denen Fenster eigentlich unnötig waren. Die Fenster eines Museums werden von den Kuratoren sowieso meistens verhängt. Ich bin natürlich nicht der erste, der das entdeckt hat. In Schinkels Museumsbauten sind die Wände auch ganz wichtig.«9

Die Mausoleum-Interpretation kontert Mario Botta folgendermaßen: »Heute haben die Menschen kein Verständnis mehr für die Bedeutung alter Baudenkmäler. Da ihre ursprüngliche Botschaft nicht begriffen wird, sind diese Gebäude heute sinnentleert. Ich würde behaupten, daß wir in diesem Fall weit entfernt sind von einer Begräbnisarchitektur. Die Stadt der Toten ist voller Symbole und wehmütiger Erinnerungen. Was im Leben nicht vollbracht wurde, wird dort vollendet.«10 Diese Aussage impliziert, daß der Architekt in seinem Museumsbau keinerlei derartigen »Symbole und wehmütigen Erinnerungen« wahrnimmt, wie sie ein Mausoleum aufweist.

Zur Vergabe des Auftrags für dieses zentral gelegene Museum mit einer Gesamtfläche von 20 900 m² schrieben die Vermögensverwalter des 1935 gegründeten San Francisco Museum of Modern Art keinen allgemeinen Wettbewerb aus, sondern führten Gespräche mit sechs Architekten: Mario Botta, Frank Gehry, Thomas Beeby, Tadao Ando, Arata Isozaki und Charles Moore. Das Museum – am 18. Januar 1995 eröffnet – befindet sich in der Nähe des Moscone Convention Center und ist Teil eines Stadterneuerungsprogramms auf 40 h, das die Stadt San Francisco bereits 1954 begonnen hatte. Das stadteigene Grundstück wurde dem SFMOMA von der Stadtentwicklungsbehörde zur Verfügung gestellt, die für den Yerba-Buena-Bezirk verantwortlich ist. Der Neubau kostete 60 Millionen US-Dollar, die fast ausschließlich durch private Spenden aufgebracht wurden. Ein zentrales *Opäum* über einem abgeschrägten Zylinder läßt Tageslicht in das fünfgeschossige Innere des Museums einfallen, vor allem in die 7 m hohen Galerieräume im oberen Geschoß.

Auf der dem SFMOMA gegenüberliegenden Straßenseite erhebt sich Fumihiko Makis Yerba Buena Center, dessen leichte, schiffsähnliche Architektur gewissermaßen im Widerstreit mit Bottas massivem fensterlosen Gebäude liegt. Da Mario Botta immer wieder unterstreicht, wie wichtig städtebauliche Qualitäten sind, mag dieser Mangel an Dialog erstaunen. »Ich möchte einen Kollegen nicht kritisieren«, sagt Botta, »aber Fumihiko Maki hat eine Art offenen Pavillon in einen Garten gebaut. Obwohl sein Gebäude an einer Straßenecke steht, öffnet es sich statt dessen auf einen Park. Ein europäischer Architekt hätte an diese Stelle einen Eckbau plaziert. Hier zeigen sich also zwei unterschiedliche städtebauliche Auffassungen. Ich halte mein Gebäude für viel urbaner, selbst wenn es geschlossen ist. Das Wort ›geschlossen‹ bedeutet in diesem Fall eigentlich nichts. Das Museum öffnet sich mit seinem monumentalen Haupteingang zur Straße hin.«11

San Francisco Museum of Modern Art

9 Ibid.
10 Ibid.
11 Ibid.

Aus einem ähnlichen Grund kritisiert Botta, daß James Stewart Polshek hinter der Bühne seines Theaterbaus an der Third Street eine hohe geschlossene Mauer errichtete, statt dort einen Eingang zu plazieren. »Für mich«, erklärt Botta, »muß in der Architektur eine Wand, selbst eine geschlossene, eine gewisse Transparenz haben. Ich muß sehen können, was sich hinter einer Mauer befindet – ein Theatersaal, eine Kunstgalerie oder ein leerer Raum. Wenn sie richtig gestaltet ist, kann eine Mauer – selbst ohne Fenster – viel ›andeutungsvoller‹ sein als Glas, das ich als das grundlegend undurchsichtigste Baumaterial überhaupt empfinde.«[12]

Auch das Museum, das Mario Botta für die Werke des Malers und Bildhauers Jean Tinguely in Basel baute (1993–1996), besitzt eine Anzahl geschlossener Fassaden. Viel kleiner als das Museum of Modern Art in San Francisco, steht es ebenfalls in einem dicht bebauten Stadtteil – auf einem Grundstück zwischen Autobahn und Rhein. Auf der Rheinseite hat Botta ein ungewöhnliches Element eingefügt, die »Barke«, eine lange gläserne, gekrümmte Fußgängerrampe, die vom Gebäude herabzuhängen scheint und Besuchern den Blick auf den Fluß erlaubt, bevor sie in die Ausstellungsbereiche gelangen. »Meine Intention dabei war«, erläutert Botta, »den Besuchern die Tatsache eindrücklich vor Augen zu führen, daß sie hier nur wenige Meter vom Rhein entfernt sind. Deshalb entwarf ich diesen ›obligatorischen‹ Zugang. Er ist eine Art Aperitif, oder eine Einführung in das Museum, die zwischen Besuchern und Stadt einen Dialog herstellen soll.«[13] Die gänzlich geschlossene Mauer des Museums Jean Tinguely befindet sich, der Bauauflage entsprechend, auf der Seite der Hochautobahn und schirmt Museumsbesucher gegen Lärm und ablenkendes Geschehen ab. In diesem Fall bezieht sich Mario Botta in seiner Gestaltung auf lokale Bauten, indem er das Gebäude nicht mit dem für seine Architektur typischen Ziegelstein verkleidete, sondern mit rotem Sandstein, der auch für das Basler Münster verwendet wurde.

Paradies und Hölle

Die Kathedrale von Evry (1988–1995) ist die bedeutendste Kathedrale, die seit über einem Jahrhundert in Frankreich errichtet wurde und rückte aus diesem Grund in das Zentrum kritischer Betrachtung. Viele warfen der katholischen Kirche vor, sie habe zu einer Zeit, in der viele Menschen Not leiden, 60 Millionen Francs für ein Kirchengebäude ausgegeben – zu Unrecht, denn es wurde ausschließlich aus Sonderspenden finanziert. Mit dem Bauwerk wird der Versuch unternommen, einer reizlosen Neustadt, die ohne großes städtebauliches Feingefühl errichtet wurde, einen Mittelpunkt zu geben. Tatsächlich gewinnt die Stadt Evry, im Süden von Paris gelegen, dank Bottas Schöpfung ein gewisses Maß an Kohärenz, trotz des ungewöhnlichen Erscheinungsbildes der Kathedrale.

Botta griff erneut auf die für seine Architektur typische abgeschrägte Zylinderform zurück und schuf ein Gebäude mit einer Gesamtfläche von 4 800 m² aus Stahlbeton mit Ziegelsteinverkleidungen innen und außen. Auf seinen Entwurf gehen auch die Kirchenbänke in burgundischer Eiche – für 800 Personen zu ebener Erde und für 400 bis 500 weitere auf den Galerien – sowie Altar und Taufbecken aus weißem Carrara-Marmor zurück. Mit ihrem kreisrunden Grundriß von 38,5 m Durchmesser lehnt sich die Kathedrale an die Tradition byzantinischer Kirchen wie die Grabeskirche in Jerusalem an und greift in dieser Hinsicht auf die Wurzeln des Christentums zurück. Eine außergewöhnliche dreieckige Metallrahmenkonstruktion bildet das Dachgestühl und läßt viel Tageslicht ins Kircheninnere dringen, was eine angenehme Raumstimmung erzeugt – wenn es auch nicht so offensichtlich »vom Geist erfüllt« wirkt wie etwa Tadao Andos Kapellen.

Einige Betrachter fühlen sich beim Anblick der Kathedrale von Evry mit ihrer Baumreihe auf der Höhe des Obergeschosses an das Haupt Christi mit der Dornenkrone erinnert. »Daran

Museum Jean Tinguely

---

12 Ibid.
13 Ibid.

habe ich tatsächlich nie gedacht«, sagt Botta dazu. »Der Zylinder hat keine Fassade. Indem ich ihn schräg anschnitt, wollte ich das Dach zu einer Fassade machen. Das Bild der Dornenkrone wäre mir nie in den Sinn gekommen, weil ich von direkter Symbolik nichts halte. Die Transponierung eines Symbols in die Architektur kann leicht zur Karikatur verkommen. In dem vollkommen mineralischen Umfeld ist eine Art Garten auf diesem öffentlichen Gebäude jedoch ideal. Ich wollte ein Element einfügen, das sich im Wind bewegt. Für das San Francisco Museum of Modern Art hatte ich übrigens eine ähnliche Idee: Ursprünglich wollte ich eine Reihe von beweglichen Elementen auf das Dach setzen, so etwas Ähnliches wie Calders Mobiles.«

Watari-um Contemporary Art Gallery

Es lohnt sich, die Überlegungen nachzuvollziehen, die Botta zur Entscheidung für die Zylinderform veranlaßten, denn sie sind der Schlüssel zum Verständnis seiner Architektur. Selbst wenn die Bäume auf der Kathedrale nicht mit der Dornenkrone assoziiert werden sollen, könnte der Zylinder doch im Sinne von Bottas Vorstellungen vom Haus als Zufluchtsstätte interpretiert werden: Die Kirche ist als »Gotteshaus« gedacht. Könnte daher ihre runde, abgeschrägte Form nicht die letzte Zufluchtsstätte des Menschen darstellen, nämlich den menschlichen Schädel? »Jede Interpretation ist denkbar«, sagt der Architekt, »aber für mich ist die Kreisform insofern am wichtigsten, als sie die maximale Grundrißfläche bei einem Minimum an Fassadenfläche bietet. Sie ist eine kraftvolle, schwierige Form, die nur einen einzigen Mittelpunkt hat. Wie eine Sonnenuhr empfängt sie das Sonnenlicht das ganze Jahr über von Tag zu Tag unterschiedlich. Ob man es nun von außen oder von innen anschaut, ein kreisrundes Gebäude wird immer sofort verstanden. Wie Heidegger schon sagte, bewohnt ein Mensch einen Raum, sobald er sich darin orientieren kann. Wenn man die Orientierung verloren hat, befindet man sich in einem Labyrinth, und ich habe das Gefühl, daß unsere gesamte moderne Kultur sich mit wenigen Ausnahmen auf ein solches Labyrinth zubewegt. In einem normalen Einkaufszentrum werden Wegweiser und Hinweisschilder benötigt, um sich zurechtzufinden!« Hiermit gibt Botta eine tiefgründigere Erklärung darüber ab, aus welchem Grund er geometrische Figuren bevorzugt, wiederum aus dem Gedanken der Orientierung heraus: »Sich in einem Gebäude gut zurechtfinden zu können ist ein Indikator für gute Qualität«, sagt er. »Geometrie löst nicht jedes Problem, sie hilft dem Architekten jedoch zu vermeiden, daß er in den Abgrund des Labyrinths stürzt. Das Labyrinth ist die Hölle und gute Orientierung das Paradies!«[14]

Mario Bottas Bauten tragen fast durchweg seine unverwechselbare Handschrift; mit seiner Form- und Materialwahl sind sie einige der klarsten der Gegenwartsarchitektur. Bereitwillig räumt er ein, daß auch seine häufig kategorischen Statements den zahlreichen, bei jedem Bauvorhaben auftauchenden Einflußfaktoren unterworfen sind: »Zugegebenermaßen kann nicht alles, was ich baue, nur das Ergebnis der strengsten Auslegung meiner Entwurfsgedanken sein, aber selbst pragmatische Entscheidungen können eine gewisse Kontinuität ermöglichen. Die Sprache meiner Architektur ist in mir. Picasso verwendete das gleiche Vokabular, um zwei sehr unterschiedliche Werke zu schaffen, die ›Demoiselles d'Avignon‹ und ›Guernica‹. Die gleichen Zeichen können eingesetzt werden, um entweder eine Liebeserklärung zu formulieren oder aber die ethische Forderung: ›Du sollst nicht töten‹. Ich erkenne den Schreibstil von Gabriel García Márquez oder die Symbole eines Paul Klee, die das Kind ansprechen, das in uns allen steckt. Giacometti hat sich oft gefragt, warum er immer wieder den ›gleichen‹ Kopf schuf, warum er nicht genau das zustande brachte, was er eigentlich vorhatte. Ich anerkenne Tadao Andos Stil. Wir haben ähnliche Absichten, selbst wenn wir ein anderes Vokabular verwenden. Er baut in Beton, aber wir beide haben die gleichen Anliegen und Ansichten über Licht und Materialien.«

14 Ibid.

Das Rätsel Stadt

Städtebauliche Fragen spielen im Werk Mario Bottas immer wieder eine Rolle. Ob in San Francisco, Basel oder der Kleinstadt Evry – Botta versucht stets, die jeweilige gebaute Umgebung zu berücksichtigen und deren Gefüge »zu verstärken«, wie er es ausdrückt. Man kann sagen, daß sein Engagement für kraftvolle urbane Statements in klar gegliederten, »ordentlichen« Schweizer Städten wie Lugano oder Basel ein relativ leichtes Spiel hat. Selbst der Yerba-Buena-Bezirk von San Francisco ist im Stadtplan streng orthogonal gerastert und bot sich an für die Fluchtung, die der Architekt für den Eingang an der Third Street konzipierte. Kann eine derartige Striktheit auch mit einem komplexeren oder chaotischeren städtischen Umfeld koexistieren? Mario Botta sagt, sie kann es, und zitiert als Beleg seine Galerie für Gegenwartskunst, Watari-um, in Tokio (1985–1990). Die Galerie steht mit ihren für Botta charakteristischen massiven Mauern und ihrer von geometrischen Überlegungen bestimmten Gestalt auf einer sehr kleinen dreieckigen Fläche von nur 157 m², inmitten einer Stadt mit einer extrem ungeordneten Struktur.

In einem Brief an die Auftraggeberin erläutert der Architekt seinen Entwurf: »Ich wurde in einem kleinen Dorf – zwischen Mailand im Süden und den Schweizer Alpen im Norden gelegen – geboren. Schon in meiner Kindheit – als die imaginäre Welt noch sehr real war – träumte ich in meinem Dörfchen von der Unendlichkeit ferner Großstädte. Noch heute verfolge ich mit Vorliebe die gleichen intensiven Empfindungen und Gefühle, die mir durch die Jahre meiner Kindheit geholfen haben. Tokio verstärkt die Widersprüche der ›modernen‹ Stadt. An jeder Straßenecke ist der Kontrast hinsichtlich Maßstab und Raum zum vorherigen kontextuellen Zustand physisch wahrnehmbar. Neben den Wunden, die von Neubaumaßnahmen geschlagen werden, überlebt ein dichter städtischer Bestand, dessen präindustrielle Matrix Erinnerungen an räumliche Beziehungen bewahrt, die heute in direktem Widerspruch zur neuen Architektur stehen. Im Babel der täglich wechselnden städtischen Formensprachen wollte ich die ›Haltbarkeit‹ eines starken elementaren Erscheinungsbilds testen, einen Architekturstil, der sich aus der inneren Logik des Bauwerks ergibt, aus seiner Geometrie und seinen Lichtwirkungen. Ich hoffe, liebe ›schwierige‹ Mrs. Watari, daß ›unser‹ Watari-um Jahrhunderte überdauern wird – genau wie die Bauten der Romanik.«[15]

Zunächst klingt der Wunsch Bottas, das Gebäude möge »Jahrhunderte überdauern«, recht vermessen. Tokio ist eine Stadt, die bereits zweimal in diesem Jahrhundert zerstört wurde – durch Erdbeben, Brand und Bomben; eine Stadt, in der zwar ein Nebeneinander von Alt und Neu, von Tempel und Hochhaus existiert, die sich jedoch fast täglich verändert und sich selbst beständig von neuem erschafft, ein Ort, an dem das Kurzlebige regiert. Zu hoffen, daß der 157-m²-Neubau im Herzen der Metropole diesem Schicksal entrinnen wird, ist eher ein Akt des Glaubens an die Solidität des architektonischen Entwurfs und der Konstruktion als eine vernünftige Einschätzung dessen, was die Zukunft bringen wird. Eine solche Hoffnung könnte sogar als Akt der Hybris bezeichnet werden, wenn nicht diese Ironie im Umgang mit seiner »schwierigen« Auftraggeberin mitschwingen würde.

Schließlich führt Botta seine Analyse der Galerie Watari-um in eine andere Richtung. Erklärtermaßen wollte er also »die ›Haltbarkeit‹ einer starken, elementaren Form in einer chaotischen Stadt testen«. Er erkennt aber auch, daß »es schwerer ist, als man denkt, das Chaos zu akzeptieren. Der Schweizer Bildhauer Jean Tinguely besaß die Fähigkeit, eine Art Chaos in Poesie zu verwandeln, doch war er auch ein Ausnahmekünstler.« Damit relativiert der Architekt seinen selbstbewußten Standpunkt und unterstreicht gleichzeitig, in welcher Hinsicht er von anderen Berufsgenossen unterschieden werden möchte. Viele

---

15 Brief Mario Bottas an Mrs. Watari, 5. August 1990.

zeitgenössische japanische Architekten haben sich die Idee zu eigen gemacht, daß eine Stadt wie Tokio tatsäch-lich eine höhere humangesellschaftliche Organisationsform darstelle als Städte des Westens mit ihren orthogo-nal gerasterten Stadtplänen. Diese Auffassung, die auf der mathematischen »Chaostheorie« basiert, führt manche von ihnen zu ganz anderen ästhetischen Entscheidungen als Mario Botta.

Die Stellungnahme Bottas zu den theoretischen Grundlagen seiner Architektur und seine damit verbundenen Verweise auf deren »Grundwerte« sind kaum anzufechten. Ein bewußtes Gespür für Licht und Materialien werden angeführt oder auch das Anliegen, Gebäudebesuchern die Orientierung zu erleichtern. Indem Mario Botta auf traditionelle, archetypische Entwürfe zurückgreift und grundlegende Werte aufzuspüren sucht, ohne in »postmodernes« Imitieren zu verfallen, kehrt er auch – wie er selbst betont – zu den eigentlichen Ausgangspunkten der Moderne zurück.

»Ich trete für den Gedanken ein«, so Botta, »daß Architektur sich von Natur unterscheiden muß.« Mit ihren kraftvollen geometrischen Formen und starken Mauern stehen seine Gebäude häufig im Kontrast zu anderen, selbst in einem städtischen Kontext. Wie das frühe Einfamilienhaus in Riva San Vitale können auch seine späteren Werke relativ distanziert oder sogar isoliert erscheinen. Einer »Gebärmut-ter« gleich sollen seine Häuser Schutz und Wärme bieten und das Innen klar vom Außen trennen. Botta ist der Auffassung, daß ein Großteil der zeitgenössischen Bauten verworfen werden sollte, da sie von der Faszination des Labyrinthischen und Flüchtigen inspiriert seien. Deshalb es vielleicht naheliegend, daß seine Lösungen sich nicht nur von der Natur, sondern auch von ihrer gebauten Umgebung abheben. Mario Botta gibt sich große Mühe, das urbane Gefüge zu »verstärken«, wenn er in einer Stadt baut. Sein Interesse richtet sich dar-auf, Fluchtungen zu schaffen oder bestehende Kompositionen zu vervollständigen, wie bei seinem »Ransila 1«-Projekt in Lugano (1981–1985) oder seinem Museum für moderne und zeitgenössische Kunst (1993–), das im italienischen Rovereto (Trento) entsteht.

Der Goldene Schnitt

Die Bedeutung von Mario Bottas Schaffen erklärt sich wohl am besten vom Aus-gangspunkt dieses Textes her: von der eindrucksvollen Tessiner Berglandschaft des Valle Maggia. Bottas Dorf-kirche (1986/92–1998) erhebt sich symbolhaft zwischen meist wiederaufgebauten Häusern. Sie ist offenbar zylindrisch, geht aber in eine Ellipse über. Rudolf Arnheim hat auf die Bedeutung dieser geometrischen Figuren hingewiesen: »Es ist ein schlichter Steinzylinder, ganz anders als die Formen, mit denen die Bewohner des Dorfs vertraut waren. Damit will ich nicht sagen, daß derart starke, schlichte Volumen dem Leben auf dem Lande zuwiderlaufen – man denke nur an die Futtersilos auf unseren eigenen Farmen –, aber einen solchen Zylinder als Kirche präsentiert zu bekommen, muß verblüffen. Genauer gesagt ist die Zylinderform im Schnitt elliptisch, und irgendwo über Körpergröße wird sie von einer schrägen Ebene abgeschnitten. Diese abrupte Unterbrechung einer vollkommenen Form könnte die Dörfler an die Ruinen erinnern, wie sie dastanden, nach-dem die Lawine über sie hinweggegangen war. ... Da das Dach glasgedeckt ist, richtet es das Gebäude und die Gottesdienstbesucher auf die Sonne aus, ganz in der Tradition alter Kirchen. Der geneigten Dachebene hat der Architekt darüber hinaus eine perfekte Kreisform gegeben.

Das ganze Gebäude spielt mit dem symbolträchtigen Wechsel von Ellipse und Kreis. In seinem Essay über Galilei als Kritiker der Künste erinnert Panofsky daran, daß Galilei es ablehnte, die Entdeckung seines Freundes Kepler anzuerkennen, wonach unser Planetensystem sich nicht auf einer Reihe konzentrischer Kreise bewege, sondern auf elliptischen Flugbahnen, mit der Sonne im Fokus einer dieser

Ellipsen. Die vollkommene Symmetrie des Kopernikanischen Systems nämlich entsprach der humanistischen Überzeugung, daß die Vollkommenheit Gottes sich am besten durch die perfekte Geometrie der Kugel oder des Kreises ausdrücken ließe und daher die zentrierte Rundform auch angemessen für einen Sakralbau sei.«[16]

Mario Bottas häufige Verwendung des Kreises in seiner Architektur kann auch als ein Hinweis auf seine Suche nach fundamentalen Werten gelten. Als in der Natur wie auch in der Kunst gegebene Grundform hat die geometrische Figur vielfältige Deutungen in der Psychologie der visuellen Wahrnehmung erfahren und ebenso von Beginn der Baukunst an. Kreise, von Mönchen des Zen-Buddhismus in einem einzigen Pinselschwung gezogen – japanisch: enso –, symbolisieren Leere, Harmonie und den Augenblick der Erleuchtung. Und die Ausdruckskraft der Dorfkirche von Mogno zum Beispiel hat durchaus einen Bezug zu diesem mystischen Sinngehalt.

Rudolf Arnheim, Autor des 1954 erschienenen Buchs »Art and Visual Perception«, definiert darin den Kreis als die elementarste Form überhaupt: »Man hat behauptet, das Kind erhalte die Inspiration zu seinen frühesten Formen von verschiedenen runden Objekten in seiner unmittelbaren Umgebung. Ein Psychoanalytiker leitet sie, nach Freud, von den Brüsten der Mutter ab, ein anderer, nach Jung, vom Mandala. Andere verweisen auf Sonne und Mond. Diese Spekulationen basieren auf der Überzeugung, daß jedes Formenmerkmal von Bildern auf irgendeine Art aus Beobachtungen der materiellen Welt gewonnen wurde. Tatsächlich genügt die grundlegende Tendenz zum einfachsten Gebilde im motorischen und visuellen Verhalten vollkommen, um die Vorrangstellung kreisrunder Erscheinungen zu erklären. Der Kreis ist das im Bildmedium einfachste verfügbare Element, weil er – auf seinen Mittelpunkt bezogen – in alle Richtungen symmetrisch ist.«[17] Das letzte Argument entspricht Bottas eigener Erläuterung: »Für mich ist die Kreisform am wichtigsten.«

Der französische Kunsthistoriker und Philosoph René Huyghe hat daran erinnert, daß Ernest Rutherford im Jahr 1915 die Struktur des Atoms zunächst als eine Anordnung konzentrischer Kreise darstellte, und darauf hingewiesen, daß die Menschen gelegentlich den Naturphänomenen ihre eigenen vorgefaßten Interpretationen von Geometrie übergestülpt haben, wie etwa Galileo Galilei.[18] Huyghe führt für das Auftreten von Kreisen und Ringstrukturen in der Natur als augenfälliges Beispiel die Wellen an, die von jedem Auftreffen eines Objekts auf dem Wasser ausgehen. In seiner »History of Electricity« (Geschichte der Elektrizität) unternahm der englische Theologe und Wissenschaftler Joseph Priestley im Jahr 1767 den Versuch, die Ringe zu erklären (nach ihm Priestley-Ringe genannt), welche sich infolge einer Entladung von Elektrizität auf einer Metalloberfläche bilden. Und Sir Isaac Newton beobachtete die kreisförmigen Muster der Lichtbeugung. In diesem Zusammenhang sei darauf verwiesen, daß Bottas Dorfkirche in Mogno einen elliptischen Grundriß hat und eine Apsis mit konzentrischen Bändern aus weißem Marmor und grauem Granit. All diese Beispiele und Modelle legen dar, daß der Kreis mehr ist als eine geometrische Figur. Er ist grundlegender Bestandteil von Ausdrucksformen der Natur und der menschlichen Wahrnehmung.

Insbesondere auch in der Architektur hat er weitreichende Bedeutung. In seinem Buch über den »Goldenen Schnitt« weist Matila C. Ghyka auf die Bedeutung des Kreises hin, wie Vitruv ihn im Kontext mit der Ableitung der grundlegenden Nord-Süd-Achse beschrieben hat, die für die Ausrichtung der antiken Architektur wesentlich war.[19] Davon ausgehend wurde die Unterteilung seiner Innenfläche, etwa durch Einschreibung eines Fünf- oder Zehnecks, zur Basis für die Proportionen von Bauten der römischen Antike und ägyptischer Tempel über die des Mittelalters und der Gotik bis zur Renaissance. Aus der elementaren Rundform von Bauwerken wie des Pantheons in Rom (c. 118–128 n. Chr.) oder Bramantes »Tempietto« (1502) hebt

"Cumbre de las Americas" Monument

16 Arnheim, Rudolf: »Notes on religious architecture«, op. cit.
17 Arnheim, Rudolf: »Art and Visual Perception, A Psychology of the Creative Eye«, University of California Press, Berkeley, California, 1974 (dt. Ausgabe: »Kunst und Sehen. Eine Psychologie des schöpferischen Auges«. Walter de Gruyter, Berlin/New York 1978; hier Neuübersetzung)
18 Huyghe, René: »Formes et forces, de l'atome à Rembrandt«, Flammarion, Paris 1971.
19 Ghyka, Matila C.: »Le nombre d'or. Gallimard«, Paris 1982.

sich die Anlage des Zentralraums heraus, der in der Architekturgeschichte immer wieder realisiert wurde; die Ellipse ist in ihr ebenso vertreten, beispielsweise in der Kirche S. Andrea al Quirinale (1658–1670) von Bernini.

Die Kreisgeometrie wird überzogen von verschiedenen symbolischen Bedeutungen, die sich in dem Maße entwickelten, in dem jede Zivilisation und jede Epoche ihre eigene Auslegung ersann. Im Osten, im Orient, fand sie ihren Niederschlag in *mandala*, *stupa* (buddhistische Sakralbauten zur Aufnahme von Reliquien) und *enso*, während der Nimbus hinter den Häuptern zu allen Zeiten und an vielen Orten die Heiligen bezeichnete. Eine der faszinierendsten und bedeutendsten künstlerischen Darstellungen diesbezüglich ist wohl Leonardo da Vincis Studie der Proportionen des menschlichen Körpers (1485–1490), seines »Vitruvschen Menschen«. Die »Perfektion« des Menschen wird hier als Ergebnis seiner Beziehung zur Kreisform dargestellt. Der Einbezug des Kreises bei den Versuchen, die idealen Proportionen der Architektur von denen des menschlichen Körpers abzuleiten, sind vielfach nachweisbar. Aus jüngerer Zeit – und zweifellos von größerer Bedeutung für Mario Botta – stammen Le Corbusiers Zeichnungen für den *Modulor*, die auf dem Goldenen Schnitt basieren und ebenfalls die menschliche Gestalt in zwei Kreise einschreiben. Die Abstimmung der Architektur auf die Verhältnisse der menschlichen Körpermaße sollte eine harmonische, menschlichen Bedürfnissen angepaßte Umwelt schaffen. Botta verwendet Le Corbusiers *Modulor*-Figur in vielen Zeichnungen, um seine Vorstellung von den Raumproportionen zu vermitteln.

In seinem Buch »The Dynamics of Architectural Form« schreibt Rudolf Arnheim: »Der Mensch kann die Formen der Architektur nutzen, um sich selbst als rationales Wesen zu bezeichnen, das rationale Formen erzeugt. Als solches empfindet er Zwiespältigkeit oder gar Feindschaft gegenüber den Erscheinungen der Natur und fühlt sich ihr vielleicht auch überlegen. Möglicherweise versucht er sogar, die Natur dazu zu bringen, sich diesem Ideal der Rationalität anzupassen.« Die Analyse läßt an die »Baumkrone« auf der Kathedrale von Evry denken oder an den einen einsamen Baum auf dem höchsten Punkt des »Ransila 1«-Gebäudes in Lugano. »Während er in den Gärten wandelt, die er selbst geschaffen hat«, so Arnheim weiter, »zwingt der Mensch der Irrationalität der Natur seine eigene Ordnung auf. Er kann aber auch eine Ordnung aufzeigen, die hinter dem ungeordneten Erscheinungsbild der Natur liegt. ... Wenn die ungeheure Vielfalt natürlicher Erscheinungen sich aus den unterschiedlichen Anwendungsarten der gleichen einfachen Gesetze ableitet, dann kann diese innere Gesetzmäßigkeit in der Natur möglicherweise durch die Gegenwart reiner geometrischer Körper, die nur der Mensch erdenken und bauen kann, heraufbeschworen werden. Ein Turm auf einem Hügel schafft einen Akzent, um den herum die Natur sich selbst in einer verständlichen Ordnung organisieren kann.«[20]

Ein Turm dieser Art in natürlicher Umgebung könnte sehr wohl Bottas Haus in Riva San Vitale beschreiben. »Ich vertrete die Auffassung, daß die Architektur sich von der Natur unterscheiden muß«, sagt Mario Botta. »Primärformen, das heißt die Geometrie, helfen mir, den vorhandenen Unterschied zwischen der Rationalität und Poesie der gebauten Welt und der Natur zu unterstreichen.« Und dennoch ist der Kreis als eine Primärform auch ein Teil der natürlichen Welt und hat, wie beschrieben, tiefe Bedeutung in der Kunstgeschichte, der Philosophie und der Religion. Er mag hier als Symbol für Bottas Denken stehen. Abgesehen davon, daß er auch mit den Anfängen der Architekturgeschichte verknüpft ist – der Kreis ist eine elementare Grundform, die wohl kaum im Verdacht stehen könnte, ein »Imitat« zu sein.

Und hierin tritt die Verbindung zwischen Vergangenheit und Gegenwart zutage. Die von den Begründern der Moderne anvisierte grundlegende Einfachheit und Schlichtheit stimmte in vielem

Tent for the 700th Anniversary of the Swiss Confederation

20 Arnheim, Rudolf: »The Dynamics of Architectural Form«, University of California Press, Berkeley 1977 (dt. Ausgabe: »Die Dynamik der architektonischen Form«, Köln 1980; hier Neuübersetzung).

mit den großen Werken der Architekturgeschichte überein. Die unter anderem von Gropius vertretene Forderung nach der *tabula rasa* hat allerdings wenig zur Klärung dieser Frage beigetragen. Demgegenüber ist Mario Botta nicht so sehr bestrebt, seine modernistischen Referenzen unter Beweis zu stellen, als vielmehr die Werte zu realisieren, welche auch den bedeutendsten Gebäuden vergangener Zeiten zugrunde liegen. Ob in Griechenland oder Rom, im Italien der Renaissance oder in Ronchamp (Notre-Dame-du-Haut) – es handelt sich vielfach um die Werte des Humanismus.

In jüngster Zeit haben sich nur wenige Architekten mit so gleichbleibendem Erfolg wie Botta darum bemüht, die zeitgenössische Architektur zu ihren Wurzeln zurückzuführen. Damit sind nicht die oberflächlich sichtbaren Elemente angesprochen, welche die Inspirationsquellen für postmoderne Imitate bildeten. Vielmehr handelt es sich um die Faktoren, die bis in die Ursprünge der gebauten Umwelt zurückreichen und die auch die herausragenden Initiatoren der modernen Architektur geleitet haben. Geeignete Lichtverhältnisse, eine durchdachte Bauausrichtung und die bewußte Abgrenzung des Gebauten von der umgebenden Natur – das sind Merkmale, die großen Bauwerken aller Kulturen und aller Zeiten gemein sind. Natürlich haben verschiedene Epochen eher und vor allem die Natur als Inspiration empfunden. Die gotische Architektur etwa folgt dem Leitbild des Baums, wohingegen die von Botta geschätzte romanische Architektur fester in Primärformen verankert ist. Gerade die massiven Mauern seiner Bauten sind ein Echo jener Zeit, als Gebäude für Jahrhunderte gebaut wurden, und verleihen seiner Architektur ihre besondere Qualität in einer Ära der »Leichtbauweise«.

Botta empfindet eine Affinität zu Tadao Ando, der seine Bauten vielleicht sogar noch rigoroser auf ihr wesentliches, geometrisches Betonminimum reduziert hat. Auch Ando bevorzugt starke Mauern, die den Innenraum nachdrücklich vom Außenraum trennen. Auch er schafft Zufluchtsstätten, insbesondere beim Bau eines Einfamilienhauses. Und genau wie Ando gelingt es Botta offenbar besser, kleine, ausdrucksstarke Gebäude zu konzipieren, als die gleichen Entwurfsprinzipien auf größere Bauwerke anzuwenden.

Mario Botta ist in einer Berglandschaft aufgewachsen und hat deren geistiges Erbe verinnerlicht, was ihn – mehr noch als die geographische Lage seiner Heimat – prägte. Obwohl der Architekt gelegentlich Stahl und Glas in größeren Mengen einsetzt, dominieren doch Steine als Materialien sein Werk, darunter Ziegelsteine und Beton. Selbst mit seinem Zelt für die 700-Jahrfeiern der Schweizerischen Eidgenossenschaft (1989–1991) schien der Architekt eher an die alten Überlieferungen nomadischer Völker erinnern zu wollen, als Konzessionen an die Schnellebigkeit unserer Tage zu machen. Das Zelt von der Form einer Kuppel war mit den Fahnen der 26 Schweizer Kantone beflaggt. Es hatte seinen Platz im Castelgrande von Bellinzona, als sei es Teil eines archaischen Entwurfs. Die Behauptung, Mario Bottas Werk sei modern und dennoch fest in der Geschichte verankert, besagt somit, daß er als Architekt seinen eigenen Weg gefunden hat.

Pierre, lumière et raison

La route qui mène à Mogno, dans la vallée de Maggia, serpente à travers quelques-uns des plus beaux paysages de la Suisse méridionale. De très ancienne tradition, l'architecture de pierre grossièrement taillée de cette région est inattendue. La Maggia est l'une des principales rivières qui alimentent le lac Majeur, et les pierres des lits des rivières et des carrières locales sont célèbres pour leur qualité. Avec ses falaises dentelées et ses cascades spectaculaires, la Valle Maggia en été est un paradis bucolique, un monde en soi. Aux confins de la vallée se trouve le petit village de Mogno, qui semble à des années lumière de toute violence. Et pourtant un inquiétant talus de terre, aujourd'hui recouvert d'herbe se projette vers les constructions à partir des vertigineuses montagnes qui les dominent : c'est la trace la plus visible de la double avalanche qui a détruit le bourg le 25 avril 1986. Au pied de cette masse terreuse, l'église Saint-Jean-Baptiste récemment achevée, remplace l'édifice du XVIIe siècle qui s'élevait au même endroit jusqu'à la nuit fatale.

La mesure du sens de ce lieu a été donnée par Rudolf Arnheim, Professor Emeritus en psychologie de l'art, Harvard University, et célèbre spécialiste de la psychologie de l'art, qui présente ainsi le symbolisme de l'architecture : « Toute œuvre d'art digne de ce nom est symbolique, et les œuvres architecturales ne font pas exception. Par symbolisme, j'entends que ces œuvres, en dehors de leurs fonctions physiques, c'est-à-dire abriter, protéger et faciliter les activités de leurs utilisateurs, véhiculent à travers leur apparence visible la signification philosophique et spirituelle de leurs fonctions. ... Cette signification symbolique n'est pas seulement une attribution appliquée au bâtiment par quelque penseur ‹ extérieur ›, une sorte d'interprétation supplémentaire, mais c'est la nature et l'essence même de sa conception. ...

En dessinant le nouveau lieu de culte [pour Mogno], Mario Botta a évité les effets paralysants des symboles fermés de l'architecture ecclésiale traditionnelle. Son église est moderne, différente au point de choquer, mais ne recherche en aucune façon la nouveauté sensationnelle. Au contraire, elle aspire à répondre à ce que l'on attend d'un temple, et trouve simplement et sans détour ses réponses dans l'expressivité de formes géométriques basiques. L'église de Botta tend vers le ciel, et répond au souhait d'Alberti qu'un lieu de culte soit ‹ isolé, et s'élève au dessus de l'environnement du quotidien. › »[1]

Ce symbolisme de l'église de Mogno touche au cœur de l'œuvre de Mario Botta, né à Mendrisio (canton du Tessin) en 1943 : « Je suis né en Suisse italienne, mais d'un point de vue culturel, je me sens plus italien que suisse. La culture de l'Italie m'a nourri, et l'on peut même dire qu'elle fait partie intégrante de mes chromosomes. Ma connaissance de l'architecture passe à de nombreux égards par des églises. L'histoire de l'architecture que je connais est celle des églises, du style roman à Ronchamp. En fait la culture méditerranéenne repose en grande partie sur les églises. Quatre-vingt-dix pour cent de ce que nous connaissons et avons retenu du Roman, de la Renaissance ou du Baroque sont liés aux bâtiments religieux. Bien entendu, la période moderne est plus vouée aux édifices civils, mais on a toujours ses dettes cachées. »[2]

Le langage des pierres

Recouvert de bandeaux alternés de marbre blanc de Peccia et de granit gris de Riveo, l'église de Mogno fait appel à des formes géométriques – cercle, ellipse et cylindre tronqué – qui ont suscité de longues discussions parmi les habitants de la région, d'esprit plus conservateur. Ce n'est pas pour autant la froide géométrie du modernisme qui vient à l'esprit. Un crucifix de bois du XVIIIe siècle est ainsi suspendu au-dessus d'une ouverture en arc derrière un autel de bois dessiné par Botta. Le lourd appareillage de pierres grises et blanches évoque néanmoins les dettes dont parle Botta. Aussi contemporaine soit-elle, l'église

Church of Saint John the
Baptist, Mogno

1 Arnheim, Rudolf : « Notes on religious architecture. » in: *Languages of design – Formalisms for Word, Image and Sound*. Volume I, Numéro 3, août 1993, Elsevier Publishers, Amsterdam.
2 Entretien de l'auteur avec Mario Botta, Lugano, 16 août 1998.

de Mogno est ancrée dans un passé lointain. « Je crois fermement », aime à dire l'architecte, « que mes racines et mon amour pour cette profession, viennent de l'architecture du Moyen Âge, du Roman et peut-être également de l'expression architecturale vernaculaire. La pérennité de l'architecture de la Valle Maggia est exemplaire. Elle va au-delà du style ou de la mode, au-delà même de la culture proprement locale. C'est un archétype. »3

Cymbalista Synagogue

Cette église n'est pas la seule conçue par Mario Botta. Une autre chapelle s'élève au sommet d'une montagne du Tessin, plus proche encore de Lugano. À la fin des années 80, le débat sur le projet de Mogno avait été intense, et s'il n'avait pas manqué de défenseurs, beaucoup pensaient qu'il était inadapté à un village montagnard. L'un des plus actifs soutiens de l'architecte avait été Egidio Cattaneo, propriétaire d'une remontée mécanique proche du grand axe routier Lugano à Bellinzona. C'est à l'arrivée de cette remontée, à 2 000 m d'altitude près du sommet du Monte Tamaro, qu'il demanda à Botta de lui construire une chapelle en souvenir de sa femme décédée. Jouissant d'une vue ininterrompue sur la vallée de Lugano, cette réalisation est l'une des œuvres les plus spectaculaires de l'architecture contemporaine. Sa puissance brute se caractérise à la fois par ses formes massives, et un étonnant parement de porphyre rugueuse. L'ensemble est complété par un cycle de fresques dues au peintre italien Enzo Cucchi, qui semble s'être trouvé en accord parfait avec la nature inspirée du propos de l'architecte. La chapelle et son décor sont indiscutablement modernes, et semblent cependant jaillir de formes beaucoup plus anciennes.

Lorsqu'on lui demande s'il est d'esprit religieux, Botta répond : « J'ai ce que l'on pourrait appeler une conception séculaire de la religion. Je crois sincèrement que l'architecture peut créer des émotions. Elle peut nous donner le désir de valeurs spirituelles, comme le silence. Le silence est le langage des pierres. Le silence est très rare dans le monde moderne, mais on peut encore le trouver dans les salles de concert et les églises. J'aime les églises parce qu'elles vous font sentir que vous participez à quelque chose. Vous êtes plus qu'une simple ombre. En fait, lorsque vous entrez dans une église, vous devriez vous sentir au centre du monde. Je pense que cette idée du sacré correspond à un besoin primordial de l'homme. Ce qui est sacré est à part, et le geste fondateur de l'architecture est de franchir une limite, de créer un espace. Son intérieur doit nécessairement être différent de son extérieur. Ainsi le concept de sacré est-il implicite dans les origines mêmes de l'architecture. Créer l'architecture est un acte sacré parce qu'il différencie notre condition d'une autre. J'aime l'architecture ancienne qui reste capable de résister, d'affronter le monde extérieur par ses propres moyens, et non pas ceux de l'électricité ou d'un rideau d'air chaud. »4

Que ce soit par amour du passé, ou parce qu'il est convaincu que l'intérieur et l'extérieur doivent être distincts, il est certain que Mario Botta donne une grande importance aux murs dans ses constructions. Ils sont ouvertement épais et lourds, coulés en béton ou revêtus de brique. Ils marquent une frontière tactile, une limite, qui, comme il le précise, « sépare un état d'un autre ». À cet égard, il se distingue d'une bonne partie de l'architecture contemporaine, qui recherche au contraire à confondre l'intérieur et l'extérieur, où à minorer la signification du mur. L'œuvre de Mario Botta est presque diamétralement opposée aux créations architecturales présentées dans la récente exposition du Museum of Modern Art à New York intitulée « Light Construction », qui mettait en avant des architectes comme Kazuo Sejima ou Herzog & de Meuron. Bien que Botta soit pragmatique quand il le faut dans l'art de la construction, et admette qu'un architecte doit s'adapter aux contraintes du projet, l'épaisseur même de ses murs illustre la remarquable constance de son style depuis les débuts de sa carrière. Dans une période d'architecture éphémère – comme il le fait remarquer – cette caractéristique lui a même valu le reproche d'avoir perdu le contact avec notre époque.

3 Ibid.
4 Ibid.

Même s'il affiche un intérêt pour le style roman ou l'architecture vernaculaire et le désir d'un retour à certaines valeurs fondamentales (voir pages suivantes), Botta doit beaucoup au mouvement moderne. Il fait ainsi remarquer que les fondateurs du modernisme partageaient de nombreuses valeurs qu'il défend aujourd'hui. « L'architecture », commente-t-il, « est l'art d'organiser l'espace. C'est si évident que l'on semble l'avoir oublié. Dans une culture de consommation et d'éphémère, il ne reste qu'une caricature d'architecture. En revenant aux valeurs essentielles, je crois que nous pouvons contribuer au progrès de la modernité, telle que Le Corbusier, Alvar Aalto ou Louis Kahn l'avaient imaginée. Leur réponse à la société industrielle se faisait en termes de besoins essentiels de l'homme. Malgré les critiques dont son œuvre est actuellement l'objet, Corbu a été l'un des rares hommes de ce siècle à avoir compris des choses aussi basiques que les saisons ou le cycle du soleil. Ce sont les seuls éléments qui demeurent. Le reste disparaît comme un feu de papier. L'héritage des modernes qui m'intéresse est la question de l'éthique du bâti, le besoin de répondre à tout prix aux besoins réels. »[5]

Même les esprits les moins religieux peuvent ressentir que la chapelle de Sainte-Marie-des-Anges, près du Monte Tamaro est un lieu d'exception. Tel un long et étroit parapet à la limite du monde, elle conduit le visiteur à une petite plate-forme où il se retrouve pratiquement seul être vivant. Même ceux qui doutent ne peuvent qu'être amenés à réfléchir, suspendus au-dessus de cette spectaculaire vallée, ou en contrebas, lorsqu'ils entrent dans la chapelle, où les énormes mains peintes par Enzo Cucchi derrière l'autel accueillent les fidèles. Nous sommes là en présence de la matrice originelle, du cœur sacré, au centre de toutes choses. Avec sa curieuse forme arquée et son revêtement de pierre brute, la chapelle se dresse, témoin de temps oubliés ou annonciatrice de temps à venir, face aux courants profonds qui nourrissent tout être humain, homme ou femme. Ce que certains appellent spiritualité pourrait être qualifié ici d'humanité. Les deux sont présentes en ce lieu. À Mogno et sur le Monte Tamaro, Mario Botta a créé des formes puissamment évocatrices, qui tirent en partie leur inspiration de l'architecture du passé. Lieu d'adoration et de prière, ces bâtiments semblent empreints d'une spiritualité non spécifiquement catholique, peut-être parce qu'ils n'ont pas adopté les formes écclésiales typiques. Ceci tient éventuellement à ce que Botta appelle son « concept séculier de la religion », mais touche également aux enjeux centraux de la fonction de l'architecture.

Sur ce sujet, les commentaires de Mario Botta sont particulièrement éclairants : « Je suis de plus en plus convaincu que l'architecte travaille dans le territoire de la mémoire. Je crois que beaucoup d'aspects fonctionnels sont en fait éphémères. Mon travail sur les églises m'a aidé à revenir aux valeurs essentielles de l'architecture qui sont la gravité, la lumière, les matériaux et les formes, structurés de façon à créer un dialogue. Construire une église comme celle de Mogno aujourd'hui, est un acte de résistance contre

Swisscom Administration Center

la culture de l'éphémère. Tout ce qui n'est pas essentiel doit être éliminé. C'est une attitude que je crois partager avec un certain nombre d'architectes contemporains comme Tadao Ando ou, dans un style différent, Alvaro Siza. C'est plus une question d'éthique que d'esthétique. »[6]

Le mur et le cercle

La réputation de Mario Botta repose à l'origine sur de spectaculaires résidences privées qui, très souvent, se détachent fortement de leur environnement. De composition

5 Ibid.
6 Ibid.

géométrique puissante, elles évoquent parfois des fortifications. Sa maison de Riva San Vitale (1971–1973) fait penser à une tour à laquelle on accède de l'arrière, par une passerelle métallique. Plus récemment, sa maison de Daro-Bellinzona (1989–1992) a été traitée comme une sorte de coin fiché au flanc d'une colline, et rappelle, là encore, une architecture défensive. Il conteste cette interprétation « militaire » de son travail, au profit d'une autre, plus physiologique : « La maison est intimement reliée à l'idée d'abri. Une caverne creusée dans la roche est comme le ventre maternel. C'est le concept de maison que je défends. Lorsque je suis fatigué du monde, je veux rentrer chez moi. Là je peux reconstituer mon énergie pour me préparer aux batailles à venir. Aussi long-temps que l'homme ressentira le besoin d'une maison, l'architecture existera. La maison que j'ai construite à Morbio, par exemple, est en partie creusée dans la montagne. C'est une caverne qui s'ouvre vers le ciel. La caverne et le ciel. L'architecture défensive est pensée pour un combat physique. Une maison devrait être comme le ventre d'une mère. »[7]

Single Family House, Riva San Vitale

Que ce soit dans ses résidences privées ou dans des constructions plus impor-tantes, le vocabulaire préféré de Mario Botta est géométrique (ronds, carrés et rectangles), nécessairement géométrique. Curieusement, en décrivant son concept de maison, il trace une forme libre, plus évocatrice d'un ventre que de ce qu'il réalisera. Interrogé sur son insistance à n'utiliser qu'un vocabulaire formel limité, il répond avec vivacité : « Je suis assez tolérant pour dire que j'aime même le travail d'Alvar Aalto! Ce que je défends, c'est l'idée que l'architecture doit se distinguer de la nature. Les formes primaires, la géométrie, m'aident à mettre en valeur la différence qui existe entre la raison, la poésie du bâti et la nature. Le concept ‹ d'architecture organique › mélange tout. S'il n'y a plus de nature, il n'y a plus de culture. Les châteaux et les clochers du passé sont à l'évidence des œuvres de l'homme. La monumentalité et la géométrie que je recherche reposent sur cette simple observation. Pour moi, ce n'est pas une question de style, mais celle de l'un des grands langages de l'architecture. »[8]

De son point de départ – le canton du Tessin – Mario Botta a progressé pour atteindre à une reconnaissance internationale à travers, plus récemment, de grands édifices comme le San Francisco Museum of Modern Art ou la cathédrale d'Evry. Bien que certains éléments stylistiques, tels le voca-bulaire géométrique ou l'utilisation de la brique, soient conservés, les constructions à grande échelle posent des problèmes différents, en particulier lorsqu'elles s'insèrent dans un contexte urbain. On peut se demander, par exemple, si la nature assez fermée de ses bâtiments leur permet réellement de participer à la continuité de la vie urbaine. L'architecte réfute naturellement cette critique.

Situé sur Third Street, dans le centre de San Francisco, le Museum of Modern Art (1989–1995) est un vaste bâtiment de 60 x 83 m de surface, et de 44 m de hauteur. Il est recouvert de panneaux de béton préfabriqués parés de brique. Mario Botta a déclaré : « Dans une ville contemporaine, le musée s'élève au statut d'une cathédrale nouvelle, à celui de lieu de mémoire et de relations avec les autres époques à travers les œuvres d'art présentées. Mais c'est également un centre d'attraction pour l'animation urbaine. Aujourd'hui plus que jamais, son rôle revêt une grande importance dans un contexte urbain de moins en moins construit selon un concept unique, de plus en plus par assemblage. » Le caractère fermé des façades, ainsi que la curieuse monumentalité du bâtiment lui donnent cependant un aspect presque funéraire. « Les façades sont très fermées », fait remarquer Botta, « parce qu'en fait nous n'avons pas besoin de fenêtres. Je cherchais au contraire une idée de mur, avec une fente unique en son milieu. J'ai donné la priorité aux intérieurs qui n'avaient guère besoin de fenêtres. Lorsque vous placez des ouvertures dans un musée, les

7 Ibid.
8 Ibid.

conservateurs s'empressent généralement de les obstruer. Je ne suis pas le premier à avoir découvert ce phénomène, bien entendu. Dans les musées de Schinkel, les murs ont une grande importance. »9

À la critique « funéraire » Botta réplique : « Aujourd'hui, les gens ne comprennent plus vraiment la signification des monuments anciens. Comme leur message original n'est plus compris, ils sont vidés de leur substance. Je maintiens qu'à cet égard, nous sommes loin ici d'une architecture funéraire. La cité des morts est emplie de symbolisme et de nostalgie. Ce qui n'a pas été accompli pendant la vie s'y réalise. »10 Il est implicite que l'architecte ne ressent aucun « symbolisme et nostalgie » d'architecture funéraire dans la conception de son musée.

Ce musée de 20 900 m² n'a pas véritablement fait l'objet d'un concours. Le conseil d'administration du San Francisco Museum of Modern Art, organisme créé en 1935, a préféré la formule de l'entretien avec six architectes de son choix : Mario Botta, Frank Gehry, Thomas Beeby, Tadao Ando, Arata Isozaki et Charles Moore. Situé près du Moscone Convention Center, il a ouvert ses portes le 18 janvier 1995 et fait partie d'un programme de rénovation urbaine de plus de 40 hectares, envisagé dès 1954 par la commune de San Francisco. Construit sur un terrain municipal mis à la disposition du SFMOMA par l'agence de rénovation responsable du quartier de Yerba Buena, cette construction a coûté 60 millions de dollars, essentiellement apportés par des donations privées. Un *oculus* central en forme de cylindre tronqué visible de l'extérieur fournit la lumière aux cinq niveaux du bâtiment, et en particulier aux galeries de 7 m de haut du niveau supérieur.

Le SFMOMA est situé de l'autre côté de la rue du Yerba Buena Center conçu par Fumihiko Maki, dont le style paquebot et léger semble en opposition avec la structure massive et sans fenêtre de Botta. En fait ces bâtiments édifiés par deux des plus célèbres architectes internationaux du moment n'ont guère de points communs. Comme il se trouve que Mario Botta insiste beaucoup sur l'importance des valeurs urbaines, ce manque de dialogue peut sembler surprenant. « Je ne veux pas critiquer un collègue », précise-t-il, « mais Maki a construit une sorte de pavillon ouvert dans un jardin. Bien qu'il soit situé à un angle de rues, il s'ouvre en fait sur un parc. Inutile de dire qu'un architecte européen l'aurait dessiné comme un bâtiment d'angle. Deux visions différentes de l'urbanisme se confrontent ici. Je considère que mon musée est beaucoup plus urbain, même s'il est fermé. Le mot ‹ fermé › ne signifie rien ici. Le Musée et sa porte monumentale font face à la rue. »11 De la même façon, Botta critique James Stewart Polshek pour avoir placé le grand mur aveugle qui ferme la scène de son théâtre sur Third Street, au lieu d'ouvrir l'entrée à cet endroit. « Pour moi », conclut-il, « le mur, même aveugle, doit posséder une certaine transparence. Je peux voir ce qui se trouve derrière un mur – un théâtre, une galerie d'art ou un espace vide. Un mur, lorsqu'il est bien dessiné, peut être beaucoup plus évocateur de ce qu'il masque que le verre, qui pour moi est le matériau de construction le plus fondamentalement opaque. »12

Le musée conçu par Mario Botta pour abriter l'œuvre de l'artiste Jean Tinguely à Bâle (1993–1996), offre également plusieurs façades fermées. Bien qu'il ne soit pas aussi vaste que le San Francisco Museum of Modern Art, il se trouve lui aussi dans un environnement urbain très dense, bloqué d'un côté par une importante autoroute. Une autre façade domine le Rhin, et c'est précisément ici que Botta a choisi d'ajouter un élément inhabituel. La « Barca » est une longue passerelle incurvée qui part en suspension du bâtiment, et offre au visiteur une vue sur le fleuve, avant de pénétrer dans le bâtiment. « Lorsque j'ai conçu ce musée », explique l'architecte, « je voulais que les visiteurs réalisent qu'ils ne se trouvaient qu'à quelques mètres du Rhin. C'est pourquoi j'ai dessiné cette entrée ‹ obligatoire › vers les espaces d'exposition. C'est une sorte de ‹ mise en bouche ›, une introduction au musée, qui a pour but de créer un dialogue entre le visiteur et

San Francisco Museum of Modern Art

9 Ibid.
10 Ibid.
11 Ibid.
12 Ibid.

la ville. »[13] La façade la plus neutre du Musée Jean Tinguely fait face à l'autoroute surélevée, et isole les visiteurs du bruit et des vues qui pourraient les distraire. Botta fait ici également un geste envers l'architecture locale en parant les murs non de sa brique habituelle, mais d'un grès rouge qui rappelle celui de la cathédrale de la ville.

Paradis et enfer

Étant le plus important des édifices religieux construits en France depuis plus d'un siècle, la cathédrale d'Evry (1988–1995) ne pouvait que faire parler d'elle. Beaucoup ont reproché à l'Église catholique d'avoir dépensé 60 millions de francs pour ce bâtiment à une époque où tant de gens sont dans le besoin, mais le projet a été entièrement financé par des donations. La cathédrale tente de donner un centre à une ville nouvelle, créée sans grand sens urbanistique. Située au sud de Paris, Evry a quelque peu renforcé sa cohérence grâce au projet de Botta, même si l'aspect de cette cathédrale semble à de nombreux habitants bien curieux.

Reprenant la forme de cylindre tronqué qui a la faveur de l'architecte, ce lieu de culte de 4 800 m² est en béton armé recouvert de 800 000 briques toulousaines, aussi bien à l'intérieur qu'à l'extérieur. Les bancs, sur lesquels peuvent prendre place 800 fidèles au rez-de-chaussée, et 400 ou 500 de plus dans les tribunes, sont en chêne de Bourgogne. De même que l'autel de marbre de Carrare blanc et les fonts baptismaux, ils ont été dessinés par l'architecte. L'inhabituel plan circulaire de 38,5 m de diamètre renvoie aux églises byzantines (par exemple à Saint-Sépulcre, Jérusalem) et donc aux origines de la chrétienté. Un cadre métallique triangulaire supporte la structure du toit qui laisse passer une généreuse lumière naturelle, rendant l'intérieur très agréable même s'il n'est pas aussi fortement nimbé de spiritualité que les chapelles d'Ando par exemple.

Avec son cercle d'arbres plantés en bordure du toit, la cathédrale évoque pour certains la couronne d'épines du Christ. « Honnêtement, je n'y ai jamais pensé », répond Mario Botta. « Le cylindre ne possède pas de façade. En le découpant dans un angle, je voulais transformer le toit en une sorte de façade. Je n'ai jamais pensé à la couronne d'épines, parce que je ne crois pas au symbolisme direct. Une transposition symbolique en architecture peut très facilement tomber dans la caricature. Dans un environnement entièrement minéral, créer une sorte de jardin au sommet de ce bâtiment public était une solution idéale. Je souhaitais ajouter un élément qui puisse réagir au vent. En fait j'avais eu une idée similaire pour le musée d'art moderne de San Francisco pour lequel j'avais proposé à l'origine un certain nombre de structures mobiles pour le toit, un peu comme des Calder. »

Le raisonnement qui a mené l'architecte à la forme circulaire d'Evry fournit une des clés de la compréhension de son œuvre. Cette forme peut s'interpréter à la lumière de son concept de maison-abri. Puisque l'église est la maison de Dieu, la forme ronde et tronquée ne symbolise-t-elle pas l'abri ultime, le crâne humain? « Toute interprétation est possible », répond l'architecte, « mais pour moi, la forme ronde est la plus essentielle. C'est la solution qui offre le maximum de surface au sol pour un minimum de surface de façade. C'est une forme puissante, difficile, qui ne possède qu'un seul centre. Comme un cadran solaire, elle reçoit la lumière du soleil de façon différente chaque jour de l'année. Que vous le voyiez de l'extérieur ou de l'intérieur, vous comprenez immédiatement un bâtiment en rond. Comme le disait Heidegger ‹ Un homme habite un espace dès qu'il est capable de s'orienter. › Si vous ne pouvez pas vous orienter, c'est que vous êtes dans un labyrinthe, et mon sentiment est que toutes les cultures modernes, à quelques rares exceptions près, s'orientent vers cette direction. Dans un centre commercial ordinaire, vous avez besoin de panneaux pour vous orienter! » Mario Botta ajoute ici une explication plus profonde encore de son attachement aux formes géométriques, toujours lié à cette nécessité de s'orienter. « Permettre de savoir où vous vous trouvez est une grande qualité pour

Evry Cathedral

13 Ibid.

Gottardo Bank

un espace bâti. La géométrie ne résout pas tous les problèmes, mais elle peut permettre à l'architecte d'éviter de tomber dans les abysses du labyrinthe. Le labyrinthe est un enfer. L'orientation est un paradis. »[14]

Dans presque tous les cas, il n'est guère difficile d'identifier une œuvre de Mario Botta. Par le choix de ses matériaux comme celui de ses formes, il a su créer l'une des « signatures architecturales » les plus lisibles de l'architecture contemporaine. Il est prêt à admettre que ses déclarations souvent catégoriques sont soumises aux nombreuses influences qui jouent sur tout projet de construction. « Tout ce que je fais ne peut être dicté par l'interprétation la plus stricte de mes idées, mais même les décisions les plus pragmatiques ne s'opposent pas à une certaine continuité. Le langage de mon architecture est en moi. Picasso s'est servi du même langage pour créer deux œuvres très différentes, les ‹ Demoiselles d'Avignon › et ‹ Guernica ›. Les mêmes signes peuvent aussi bien servir à une déclaration d'amour qu'à une proclamation éthique selon laquelle les hommes ne doivent pas s'entretuer. Je peux reconnaître le style de Gabriel García Márquez, ou la symbolique d'un Paul Klee qui parle à l'enfant qui est en chacun de nous. Giacometti se demandait souvent pourquoi il sculptait toujours la ‹ même › tête, pourquoi il ne pouvait faire exactement ce qu'il voulait. Je peux reconnaître le style de Tadao Ando ... Nous partageons des préoccupations similaires, même si nous nous servons d'un langage différent. Il se sert du béton, mais nous avons les mêmes préoccupations en termes de lumière et de matériaux. »

L'énigme urbaine

L'enjeu urbanistique se retrouve fréquemment dans l'œuvre de Mario Botta. Que ce soit à San Francisco, à Bâle ou dans la ville nouvelle d'Evry, il s'efforce de prendre en compte le bâti existant et, comme il l'explique, de « renforcer » son tissu. On peut dire que son engagement au profit d'expressions urbaines puissantes a trouvé un territoire relativement facile dans les villes suisses si bien ordonnées de Lugano ou de Bâle. Même San Francisco, au milieu du quartier de Yerba Buena, reste strictement orthogonal et proposait un alignement aisé sur Third Street. Une telle affirmation peut-elle coexister avec une urbanité plus complexe, voire chaotique? Botta en est persuadé, et cite en exemple sa Galerie d'art contemporain Watari-um à Tokyo (1985–1990). Implantée sur une très petite parcelle triangulaire de 157 m² au milieu d'une ville connue pour sa structure extrêmement brouillonne, elle conserve néanmoins les murs et la conception puissamment géométrique de l'architecte.

Une lettre envoyée à ses clients éclaire son point de vue : « Je suis né dans un petit village entre Milan et les Alpes du Nord. Enfant, vivant encore dans l'imagination, je rêvais dans mon hameau de l'immensité des grandes villes lointaines. Aujourd'hui, j'aime encore rechercher ces sensations et ces sentiments si intenses qui m'ont aidé pendant ces années d'enfance. Tokyo porte au plus haut les contradictions de la cité ‹ moderne. › Le contraste dimensionnel et spatial par rapport au contexte préexistant est physiquement perceptible à chaque coin de rue. Parallèlement aux blessures infligées par de nouvelles constructions, un contexte urbain dense survit. Sa matrice pré-industrielle préserve la mémoire de relations spatiales qui entrent maintenant en contraste direct avec la nouvelle architecture. Dans cette Babel de langages urbains en modification quotidienne, je voulais tester la ‹ durabilité › d'une image forte, primaire, d'une architecture générée par la logique interne du bâtiment, sa géométrie, et les effets de la lumière. Mon espoir est, chère ‹ difficile › Mme Watari, que ‹ notre › Watari-um vivra des siècles, aussi longtemps que les bâtiments romans. »[15]

Pour ceux qui connaissent bien Tokyo, le souhait de Mario Botta de voir sa réalisation « durer des siècles » peut sembler légèrement présomptueux. La ville n'a-t-elle pas déjà été détruite deux

---

14 Ibid.
15 Lettre à Mme Watari 5 août 1990.

fois au cours de ce siècle par des tremblements de terre, le feu et les bombes? Elle change presque chaque jour, se reforme constamment, règne de l'éphémère, malgré les strates historiques de tissus urbains qui sous-tendent l'ensemble. Espérer que 157 m² au cœur de la métropole pourront échapper à ce destin est plus un acte de foi dans la solidité de la conception et de la construction architecturales qu'une analyse raisonnable de ce que le futur peut réserver. On pourrait même parler de prétention. À cet égard, Mario Botta n'est bien évidemment pas le seul. Les grands architectes de notre temps ont souvent à juste titre une haute opinion d'eux-mêmes. Selon Mario Botta sa référence à la durée de vie de ce bâtiment n'était qu'une boutade.

Tamaro Chapel

Mais Botta réoriente ensuite son analyse de la Galerie Watari-um dans une direction inattendue. Comme il l'affirme, il souhaitait « tester la ‹ durabilité › » d'une forme ‹ puissante et primaire › dans une cité chaotique. « Accepter le chaos est plus difficile que vous ne le pensez », poursuit-il, « il faut être très fort pour y réussir. Le sculpteur suisse Jean Tinguely pouvait transformer une sorte de chaos en poésie, mais c'était un artiste exceptionnel. » L'architecte retourne donc à une modestie mieux séante qui n'en met pas moins en valeur la manière dont il souhaite se distinguer de ses confrères. De nombreux architectes japonais contemporains, par exemple, pensent qu'une ville comme Tokyo représente en fait un degré d'organisation humaine plus élevé que les cités occidentales orthogonales. Leur réflexion, qui repose en partie sur la théorie mathématique du chaos, n'est pas sans fondement, et les conduit à des décisions esthétiques très différentes de celles de Botta.

Les théories sous-jacentes à l'œuvre de Mario Botta, telles qu'il les exprime, sont indiscutables jusqu'à présent, de même que sa référence aux « valeurs de base » de l'architecture. Dans toute construction doit se retrouver une conscience de la lumière et des matériaux ainsi qu'un sens de l'orientation. Lorsque Mario Botta parle de l'architecture de la Valle Maggia, il évoque l'idée d'archétypes. En regardant le passé et en tentant de rechercher des valeurs fondamentales sans tomber dans un pastiche « postmoderne », il revient, comme il le fait remarquer d'ailleurs, aux bases même du mouvement moderne.

« Ce que je défends », dit-il, « est l'idée que l'architecture doit être distincte de la nature. » Ses formes géométriques puissantes et ses murs épais tendent également souvent à distinguer ses constructions de celles de ses confrères, même en environnement urbain. Comme sa première maison de Riva San Vitale, son œuvre peut sembler parfois à part, voire isolée. Telles un « ventre maternel, » ses maisons se veulent des abris qui séparent clairement l'intérieur de l'extérieur. Comme il trouve qu'une bonne part de l'architecture contemporaine, fascinée par le labyrinthe et l'éphémère, devrait être rejetée, il peut sembler naturel que son œuvre se différencie souvent non seulement de la nature, mais aussi de l'environnement construit. Mario Botta s'attache à « renforcer » le tissu urbain lorsqu'il travaille dans le cadre d'une ville. On observe un substantiel effort de sa part pour rechercher des alignements ou pour compléter des compositions existantes comme il le fait, par exemple, dans son immeuble « Ransila 1 » à Lugano (1981–1985), ou pour le futur musée d'art moderne et contemporain (et centre culturel) de Rovereto (Trente), en Italie (1993–). Mais tous les visiteurs du San Francisco Museum of Modern Art ne trouveront sans doute pas ses murs de brique aussi transparents qu'il le souhaiterait.

Le nombre d'or

La meilleure clé pour apprécier l'importance de l'œuvre de Mario Botta se trouve là encore où ce texte a commencé, dans le magnifique paysage montagneux de la vallée de Maggia. Au milieu des maisons du village pour la plupart reconstruites, l'église de Mogno (1986/92–1998) se détache telle un symbole. Bien qu'elle n'ait en rien l'aspect d'une église traditionnelle, elle s'élève d'une manière à laquelle aucun autre édifice ne peut prétendre. Apparemment construite en cercle, elle tend vers l'ellipse, formes qui possèdent leur signification propre comme Rudolf Arnheim l'a noté :

« C'est un simple cylindre de pierre, assez différent des formes auxquelles les villageois avaient été habitués. Non que ces formes simples et fortes soient étrangères à la vie rurale – on se rappelle le silo de nos fermes – mais avoir un tel cylindre comme église locale ne doit pas manquer de surprendre. Ce cylindre est plus exactement de section elliptique. Un peu au-dessus de la hauteur d'un homme, il est coupé en biais par un plan oblique. Cette interruption brutale d'une forme parfaite peut rappeler aux villageois les ruines qu'ils virent après l'avalanche ... Comme le toit est recouvert de verre, il oriente le bâtiment et l'assemblée qui s'y réunit vers le soleil, comme les églises l'on traditionnellement toujours fait. De plus, l'inclinaison de son plan prend la forme d'un cercle parfait.

Le bâtiment dans son ensemble joue sur l'interaction évocatrice de l'ellipse et du cercle. Panofsky, dans son essai sur Galilée critique artistique, nous rappelle que celui-ci avait refusé la découverte de son ami Kepler selon lequel notre système planétaire ne consistait pas en cercles concentriques, mais en trajectoires elliptiques, le soleil occupant le foyer d'une de ces ellipses. La symétrie parfaite du système copernicien correspondait à la croyance humaniste selon laquelle la perfection divine s'exprimait au mieux dans la forme géométrique parfaite de la sphère ou du cercle, et qu'ainsi la forme la plus appropriée d'un sanctuaire devait être centrée et circulaire. »[16]

En dehors de ses références aux théories de Galilée et de Kepler, l'utilisation fréquente par Mario Botta de la forme circulaire est révélatrice de la nature de sa recherche de valeurs fondamentales. Forme basique qui existe aussi bien dans la nature qu'en art, le cercle développe de vastes ramifications dans la psychologie de la perception visuelle aussi bien que dans les fondations mêmes de l'architecture. L'*enso*, le cercle dessiné d'un seul trait par les moines bouddhistes zen, symbolise le vide, l'unicité et le moment de l'illumination. Cette signification mystique n'est pas totalement sans lien avec la puissance de l'église de Mogno par exemple.

Rudolf Arnheim est surtout connu pour être l'auteur de « Art and Visual Perception », publié pour la première fois en 1954. Dans cette œuvre, il définit l'importance du cercle, forme pour lui la plus fondamentale. « Il a été établi que l'enfant trouve sa première inspiration formelle dans divers objets ronds observés dans son environnement. Le psychologue freudien y voit les seins de la mère, le jungien le mandala, et d'autres évoquent le soleil et la lune. Ces spéculations reposent sur la conviction que toute qualité formelle d'une image doit d'une certaine façon venir d'observations du monde physique. En fait, la tendance fondamentale à la forme la plus simple inhérente au comportement moteur et visuel suffit à expliquer la priorité des formes circulaires. Le cercle est la forme la plus simple du médium de l'image parce qu'il est symétriquement centré dans toutes les directions. »[17] Cette dernière remarque renvoie à l'explication de Botta lui-même : « Pour moi, la forme ronde est la plus essentielle. »

Se rappelant que Ernest Rutherford représenta en 1915 pour la première fois la structure de l'atome comme une série de cercles concentriques, l'historien d'art et philosophe René Huyghe fait remarquer que les hommes ont à l'occasion imposé leurs notions préconçues de géométrie sur les phénomènes naturels, comme l'avait fait Galilée.[18] Les cercles, en particulier concentriques, existent néanmoins fréquemment dans la nature. Huyghe cite ainsi les ondes qui irradient à partir d'un point d'impact, par exemple. En 1767, dans son « History of Electricity », le théologien et savant anglais Joseph Priestley chercha à expliquer

Gottardo Bank

16 Arnheim, Rudolf : « Notes on religious architecture. », op. cit.

17 Arnheim, Rudolf : « Art and Visual Perception. A Psychology of the Creative Eye ». University of California Press, Berkeley, Californie, 1974.

18 Huyghe, René : « Formes et forces, de l'atome à Rembrandt ». Flammarion, Paris, 1971.

les anneaux (appelés anneaux de Priestley) qui se forment à la suite d'une décharge électrique sur une surface métallique. Isaac Newton, nota également la forme circulaire de la diffraction de la lumière. On peut observer en passant que la chapelle de Botta possède un plan au sol elliptique, et une abside à bandeaux concentriques de marbre blanc et de granit gris. Le cercle est donc plus qu'une forme géométrique ou moderniste. C'est un élément fondamental des langages de la nature et de la perception.

Single Family House, Morbio-Superiore

En architecture, la signification du cercle est riche de sens. Dans son œuvre sur le ‹ Nombre d'or › Matila C. Ghyka remarque que la signification de la forme circulaire telle que la décrit Vitruve vient de l'axe nord-sud fondamental dans l'orientation des constructions de l'Antiquité.[19] À partir de là, la subdivision du cercle dans lequel s'inscrit un pentagone, ou un décagone par exemple, se trouve à la base des proportions de nombreux monuments anciens, des temples égyptiens jusqu'à Rome et même aux églises gothiques et aux bâtiments de la Renaissance. La forme ronde de bâtiments aussi connus que le Panthéon de Rome (vers 118–128) ou le « Tempietto » (1502) de Bramante montre que cette forme à plan central est présente tout au long de l'histoire de l'architecture. L'ellipse est également présente dans des édifices comme San Andrea al Quirinale (1658–1670) du Bernin.

À cette géométrie naturelle du cercle, chaque civilisation et chaque époque a ajouté ses significations symboliques propres et multiples. En Orient, le *mandala*, le *stupa* ou l'*enso* reprennent cette forme essentielle, tandis que l'auréole signale les personnages sacrés dans de nombreux endroits et époques. L'une des représentations artistiques du cercle les plus étonnantes et les plus significatives est peut-être l'étude de Léonard de Vinci sur les proportions du corps de l'homme « vitruvien » (vers 1485–1490). La perfection de l'homme s'exprime ici en relation avec le cercle. L'omniprésence du cercle dans les tentatives de déterminer les proportions idéales de l'architecture de celles du corps humain s'observe également dans les figures vitruviennes de Cesare Cesariano ou de Francesco di Giorgio. Plus près de nous, et sans doute plus signifiant pour Botta, les dessins du *Modulor* de Le Corbusier, reposent sur le nombre d'or et décrivent également le corps humain inscrit dans deux cercles. Dans beaucoup des croquis de présentation de ses projets, Mario Botta se sert du personnage corbuséen du *Modulor* pour donner une idée des proportions des espaces.

Dans son livre « The Dynamics of Architectural Form », Rudolf Arnheim écrit : « L'homme peut se servir de l'architecture pour s'affirmer son existence de créature rationnelle génératrice de formes rationnelles. Ce faisant il se sent en antinomie avec l'apparence de la nature et peut-être supérieur à elle. Il peut même entreprendre de rendre la nature elle-même conforme à son idéal de rationalité. » Cette analyse fait penser à la « couronne » de la cathédrale d'Evry ou à l'arbre solitaire perché au sommet de l'immeuble « Ransila 1 » de Lugano. « Pendant qu'il joue avec ses propres réalisations », poursuit Arnheim, « l'homme impose son ordre à l'irrationalité de la nature, il peut également révéler un ordre sous l'apparence désordonnée de celle-ci. Si toutes les choses naturelles se réduisaient en dernier lieu à cinq solides réguliers stéréométriques, comme Platon le soutient dans son ‹ Timée ›, ou si la variété de l'apparence naturelle provenait de l'application de lois simples, cette légitimité inhérente se retrouverait peut-être dans la nature à travers la présence de formes géométriques pures que seul l'homme peut concevoir et construire. Ainsi, une tour au sommet d'une colline crée un accent autour duquel la nature peut s'organiser en un ordre compréhensible. »[20]

Cette tour stéréométrique dans un cadre naturel pourrait bien ressembler à la maison de Botta à Riva San Vitale. « Je défends l'idée que l'architecture doit être différente de la nature », insiste Mario Botta. « Les formes primaires, la géométrie, m'aident à souligner la différence existant entre la raison et la

19 Ghyka, Matila C. : « Le nombre d'or ». Gallimard, Paris, 1982.
20 Arnheim, Rudolf : « The Dynamics of Architectural Forms ».
University of California Press, Berkeley, Californie, 1977.

Quinto Service Station

poésie du construit et celles de la nature. » Il reste que la forme basique par excellence du cercle, fréquemment présente dans son œuvre fait partie de l'univers naturel, et revêt des significations profondes en histoire de l'art, en philosophie et dans les religions. Le cercle peut être considéré comme un symbole de sa pensée. Substantiellement reliée aux racines mêmes de l'histoire de l'architecture, symbolique dans de nombreuses croyances du « vide, de l'unicité et du moment d'illumination, » c'est aussi une forme géométrique primaire que l'on ne peut en aucun cas suspecter d'être un pastiche.

Le lien entre le passé et le présent apparaît ici. La simplicité fondamentale recherchée par les fondateurs du modernisme est souvent en complète harmonie avec les grandes architectures du passé. La *tabula rasa* déclarée par Gropius n'a guère contribué à clarifier ce débat, mais l'œuvre de Mario Botta ne tend pas tant à prouver ses lettres de modernité qu'à rechercher les valeurs qui ont présidé à la création des grandes œuvres du passé. En Grèce, à Rome, dans l'Italie de la Renaissance, ou à Ronchamp (Notre-Dame-du-Haut), ce sont souvent des valeurs humanistes. Même lorsqu'une autre force peut être évoquée, comme au sommet du Monte Tamaro, on trouve d'abord et avant tout une approche de l'expérience humaine, inscrite dans le cercle éternel, à l'abri de murs solides.

À une époque récente, peu de créateurs ont tenté avec autant de constance que Mario Botta à faire revenir l'architecture contemporaine à ses racines. Celles-ci ne sont certainement pas celles, superficielles, qui ont inspiré les pastiches des années postmodernes. Elles remontent aux origines du bâti et traversent les fondations du modernisme. La lumière, l'orientation et la détermination à séparer l'architecture et la nature sont des éléments communs aux grandes structures de nombreuses civilisations à travers les âges, même si en d'autres lieux et à d'autres époques, la nature a pu, au contraire, devenir une source d'inspiration. L'architecture gothique fait appel à l'imagerie de l'arbre, tandis que le roman admiré par Botta s'ancre davantage dans les formes primaires. L'épaisseur même des murs de Botta, qui rappelle un temps où les constructions étaient faites pour durer des siècles, lui confèrent une place à part dans notre époque de « construction légère. »

Il se sent en affinité avec l'architecte japonais Tadao Ando qui est encore allé plus loin dans la réduction des bâtiments à leur minimum géométrique et structurel. Ando aime aussi les murs épais qui séparent clairement l'intérieur de l'extérieur. Lui aussi construit des abris, en particulier lorsqu'il dessine des maisons. Comme lui, Botta semble au mieux de son expression lorsqu'il conçoit de petites constructions puissantes plutôt que lorsqu'il applique ces mêmes principes à une échelle plus vaste.

Mario Botta est un montagnard dont l'héritage intellectuel est encore plus méridional que son lieu de naissance. Bien qu'il se serve à l'occasion d'acier et de verre, il est surtout l'homme de la pierre – de la brique et du béton. Même lorsqu'il construit une tente pour la célébration du 700ème anniversaire de la Confédération Helvétique (1989–1991), il semble vouloir se référer davantage aux anciennes traditions des peuples nomades que de concéder quoi que ce soit aux recherches à la mode sur l'éphémère. En forme de coupole et surmontée des 26 drapeaux des cantons, elle s'est intégrée dans le Castelgrande de Bellinzona, comme si elle faisait partie d'un plan très ancien. Dire que l'œuvre de Mario Botta est moderne et en même temps fermement ancrée dans le passé, c'est dire qu'il a réussi dans sa quête d'architecte.

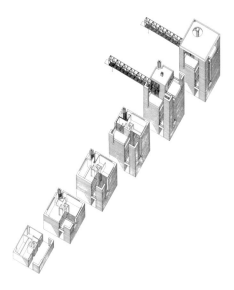

Single Family House
Riva San Vitale, Ticino, Switzerland, 1971—1973

Built on a sharply inclined hillside above the fishing village of Riva San Vitale on Lake Lugano, this 220 square meter house is set on an 850 square meter site. It has a square plan, and is built of double layers of load-bearing cement blocks. Painted white inside, the concrete block walls are complemented by terracotta floors. A red metal bridge provides the entrance passage, which resembles a fortification, an impression heightened by its relative isolation. As it may be within, the materials and the form of the house seen from the exterior convey a certain image of coldness. This may not be the point of view of the architect. "The house," says Mario Botta, "is intimately related to the idea of the shelter. A cave carved out of the rock is like a mother's womb. This is the concept of the house that I defend." Yet this house also sets out clearly Mario Botta's concept of an architecture that must differentiate itself from its natural setting.

Das Einfamilienhaus mit einer Wohnfläche von 220 m² steht auf einem 850 m² großen Grundstück am Ufer des Luganer Sees nördlich des alten Fischerdorfs Riva San Vitale. Es weist einen quadratischen Grundriß auf. Die tragenden Wände sind doppelschalige Zementsteinkonstruktionen, außen unverputzt, innen weiß gestrichen. Die Fußböden sind mit roten Terrakottafliesen belegt. Eine rotlackierte Metallbrücke führt zum Eingang des Wohngebäudes, dessen Festungscharakter durch die relativ isolierte Lage am Fuße eines Steilhangs noch unterstützt wird. Seine roh belassenen Materialien und seine streng kubische Form vermitteln dem Betrachter von außen den Eindruck von Kälte. Der Architekt vertritt jedoch eine andere Auffassung. »Das Haus ist eng verbunden mit der Vorstellung eines Zufluchtsorts«, so Mario Botta. »Eine in den Felsen gehauene Höhle ist wie ein bergender Mutterleib. Das ist das Entwurfskonzept des Hauses, das ich vertrete.« Dennoch ist das Gebäude auch ein deutlicher Beleg für Bottas Konzeption einer Architektur, die sich von ihrer natürlichen Umgebung abgrenzen muß.

Construite au flanc d'une colline escarpée qui est située au nord du village de pêcheurs de Riva San Vitale en bordure du lac de Lugano, cette maison de 220 m² s'élève sur un terrain de 850 m². Sur un plan carré, s'articulent des murs constitués d'une double épaisseur de blocs porteurs de ciment peint en blanc sur leur face intérieure, et des sols en terre cuite. Une passerelle métallique rouge permet de pénétrer dans cette maison qui évoque dans une certaine mesure une forteresse, impression que renforce son isolement relatif. Aussi confortable soit-elle, son apparence extérieure lui donne une certaine froideur, même si ce n'est certainement pas l'opinion de son architecte. Pour Mario Botta, « L'idée de maison est intimement liée à celle d'abri : une caverne creusée dans les rochers, un peu comme le ventre d'une mère. C'est le concept de maison que je défends. » Cette maison familiale illustre par ailleurs sa conviction que l'architecture doit se démarquer de son cadre naturel.

Axonometric sections of each level of the house show how its complex form is generated, beginning with the ground level, and reaching up to the bridge and roof. To the right, the house seen through the trees along the edge of Lake Lugano.

Axonometrien von jeder Etage verdeutlichen, wie sich die komplexe Form des Hauses entwickelte: ausgehend vom Erdgeschoß über die Brücke bis zum Dach. Rechts: Blick auf das Haus durch die Bäume am Ufer des Luganer Sees.

Les coupes axonométriques des différents niveaux de la maison montrent comment a été élaborée sa forme complexe, du rez-de-chaussée à la passerelle et au toit. À droite, la maison vue à travers les arbres, au bord du lac de Lugano.

VEDUTA DA SUD

MAROGGIA

LAGO DI LUGANO

A drawing and a photo (p. 44) show the entry bridge situated near the roof of the house because of the steeply sloping lakeside site. The deep notches in the side of the house (above) allow light to penetrate into living spaces (left), which are often double-height and interconnected.

Zeichnung und Foto (S. 44) zeigen die Brücke zum Eingang, der aufgrund der Lage des Hauses am Steilhang ins Obergeschoß verlegt wurde. Durch die tiefen Einschnitte in der Hauswand (oben) fällt Tageslicht in die ein- und zweigeschossigen, ineinander übergehenden Innenräume (links).

Croquis et photo (p. 44) illustrant la passerelle d'accès qui franchit l'escarpement de la rive du lac presque au niveau du toit. Les profondes découpes sur le côté de la maison (ci-dessus) font pénétrer la lumière naturelle dans les pièces de vie (à gauche), souvent à double hauteur et interconnectées.

Middle School
Morbio Inferiore, Ticino, Switzerland, 1972–1977

This large, repetitive, modular structure set on a 28,800 square meter site was commissioned by the Canton of Ticino. Much more than in later works by Mario Botta, the influence of a certain brutalism or alternatively of Italian rationalism seems to be clearly in evidence here. Although descriptive texts do refer to the school building in terms of a "subdued brutality," it is intended to outline nothing less than a "new relationship between man and the environment." A central "backbone" or promenade receives ample natural light, a continuous characteristic of the school, whose net floor area is 15,000 square meters. Using concrete frequently and blocks of porphyry on outdoor surfaces, the architect emphasizes an impression of solidity that was certainly to become one of the most recognizable hallmarks of his mature style. Aside from its windows and skylights, this building appears to make no visible concessions to its rather green and mountainous natural setting.

Auftraggeber für dieses große Schulgebäude auf einem 28 800 m² umfassenden Gelände war der Kanton Tessin. Viel stärker als bei Bottas späteren Bauten wird hier der Einfluß des Brutalismus beziehungsweise des italienischen Rationalismus deutlich. Obwohl einige Erläuterungstexte von einer »gedämpften Brutalität« sprechen, soll das Bauwerk nichts weniger als »eine neue Beziehung zwischen Mensch und Natur« umreißen. Ein zentrales »Rückgrat«, das heißt der zentrale Korridor, wird großzügig von Tageslicht erhellt, ebenso die übrigen Räumlichkeiten der Realschule, die über eine Gesamtfläche von 15 000 m² verfügt. Der Architekt verwendet für die Gestaltung der sich wiederholenden Baumodule hauptsächlich Sichtbeton, für die Außenfassaden zudem Porphyr, und betont damit den Eindruck von Solidität – eines der am deutlichsten wiedererkennbaren Merkmale seines späteren, ausgereiften Stils. Allein die Fenster und Oberlichter des Gebäudes scheinen Bottas sichtbare Konzessionen an die grüne, bergige Landschaft ringsum zu sein.

Cette vaste structure modulaire répétitive, édifiée sur un terrain de 28 800 m² est une commande du canton du Tessin. Beaucoup plus que les œuvres ultérieures de Mario Botta, elle traduit l'influence d'un certain brutalisme ou du rationalisme italien. Bien que ses descriptifs parlent de « brutalité maîtrisée », ce projet ne se proposait rien de moins que de définir « une nouvelle relation entre l'homme et l'environnement ». Une « colonne vertébrale » centrale, ou promenade, reçoit une généreuse lumière naturelle, caractéristique omniprésente de cette école primaire dont la surface au sol atteint 15 000 m². Recourant fréquemment au béton et au porphyre pour les surfaces extérieures, l'architecte met ici en valeur le sentiment de solidité qui allait devenir typique du style de sa maturité. En dehors de ses fenêtres et de ses verrières, ce bâtiment ne semble faire aucune concession visible à son cadre naturel montagneux et verdoyant.

A view into the library seen through one of the entrance doors. A large open space with ample natural light characterizes this interior area.

Blick zur Bibliothek durch eine der Außentüren (oben). Die Aula: ein großer offener Raum mit viel Tageslicht.

Vue de la bibliothèque par l'une des portes d'entrée (en haut). L'intérieur se caractérise par un vaste espace ouvert, baigné d'une généreuse lumière naturelle.

Although it is a repetitive modular structure, the Morbio Inferiore Middle School has an apparently irregular roof profile, which corresponds to the skylights along the central "backbone" of the building.

Obwohl es sich bei der Realschule in Morbio Inferiore um eine repetitive modulare Konstruktion handelt, besitzt sie ein augenfällig unregelmäßiges Dachprofil, und zwar aufgrund der Oberlichter im Dach des zentralen Korridors – des »Rückgrats« der Schule.

Malgré sa conception modulaire répétitive, le collège de Morbio Inferiore présente un profil de toit apparemment irrégulier, qui correspond aux verrières implantées le long de l'axe central du bâtiment.

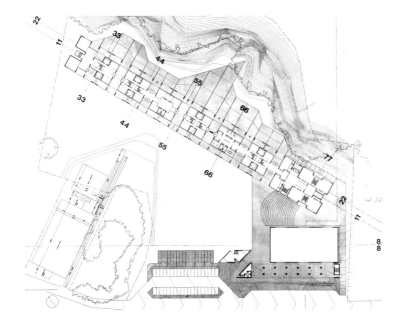

Seen against a natural backdrop, the Middle School stands out distinctly as a man-made structure, which does not seek to adapt itself specifically to its site. A plan shows how its linear concept contrasts with the highly irregular topographical profile of the nearby hills.

Vor dem Hintergrund der Landschaft hebt sich die Realschule deutlich als von Menschenhand »gebaute Umwelt« ab, die nicht versucht, sich dem Gelände in besonderer Weise anzupassen. Die lineare Entwicklung des Gebäudes steht im Gegensatz zu den unregelmäßig gezackten Silhouetten der umgebenden Berge.

Construction humaine qui ne cherche pas à s'adapter spécifiquement à son site, le collège se détache sur le fond des montagnes. Le plan montre le contraste entre le profil topographique irrégulier des collines voisines et le concept linéaire du bâtiment.

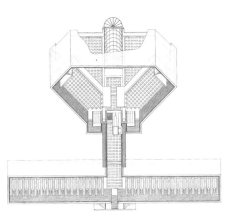

Library of the Capuchin Convent
Lugano, Switzerland, 1976–1979

Because it is set partially below ground level, this reinforced concrete addition
to a restored church of the seventeenth century is not readily visible from the exterior. With a net floor area of
900 square meters, and a volume of 3,800 cubic meters, the space includes a double-height reading room
with ample skylights. Although the plan of the addition is perfectly symmetrical, it assumes a shape that is not
frequent in Botta's architecture – essentially hexagon. A bright entrance atrium set into the vaulted space of the
older building sets the mood for the more rectilinear design of the library itself. The architect establishes a
powerful continuity in the design, and a sense of the upward-looking mission of the client, the Convent of the
Capuchins of Lugano, through such gestures as a vertical fissure in the reading room that reveals the structural
concrete, and leads the eye of the visitor toward the skylight.

Der Erweiterungsbau der restaurierten Klosterkirche des Kapuzinerordens aus
dem 17. Jahrhundert ist zum Teil unter Planum angelegt und von außen daher ziemlich unauffällig. Den Innenraum nimmt ein Lesesaal von doppelter Geschoßhöhe ein (Gesamtfläche 900 m², Volumen 3 800 m³), der mit
einem großen Oberlicht versehen ist. Der symmetrisch angelegte Bau aus Stahlbeton weist eine Form auf, die
in Bottas Architektur selten erscheint: im wesentlichen die eines Hexagons. Ein in den Gewölberaum des
älteren Komplexes eingestelltes, hell belichtetes Atrium bestimmt grundlegend die Atmosphäre der geradlinig
konzipierten Bibliothek. Der Architekt hat sie konsequent kraftvoll durchgestaltet und in seinem Entwurf die im
übertragenen, geistlichen Sinne »aufwärtsstrebende« Mission des Bauherrn – des Kapuzinerkonvents von
Lugano – in verschiedene Elemente übersetzt, etwa in einen vertikalen Einschnitt in der Wand des Lesesaals,
der den Blick des Besuchers in die Höhe, zum Licht, lenkt.

Édifiée en partie au dessous du niveau du sol, cette extension du couvent des
Capucins en béton armé d'une église du XVIIᵉ siècle restaurée est à peine visible de l'extérieur. Sur 900 m² de
surface au sol et un volume de 3 800 m³, elle comprend une salle de lecture à double hauteur éclairée par de
vastes verrières. Si le plan est parfaitement symétrique, il emprunte une forme essentiellement hexagonale, peu
fréquente chez Botta. Un atrium d'entrée très lumineux inséré sous les voûtes du bâtiment ancien donne le ton
à la conception plus rectiligne de la bibliothèque. L'architecte a atteint une puissante unité de dessin et un sens
de spiritualité qui convient à ce couvent, par des gestes comme la grande fissure verticale dans la salle de lecture qui révèle le béton structurel et oriente le regard du visiteur vers la verrière.

*To the right, the reading room
of the library, with its concrete
coffers and ample skylight.
The axonometric drawing (left,
above) shows the reading room
and library stacks as seen from
below. The original structure of
the Convent is visible in the
image above.*

*Rechts der Lesesaal der
Bibliothek mit seiner Betonkas-
settendecke und einem großen
Oberlicht. Die axonometrische
Darstellung (oben links) zeigt
Lesesaal und Bibliotheksregale
in Untersicht. Oben rechts: der
ursprüngliche Klosterbau.*

*À droite, la salle de lecture
de la bibliothèque à plafond à
caissons de béton et vaste verrière. La représentation axonométrique (en haut à gauche)
montre, vue du dessous, la salle
de lecture et les réserves. Ci-
dessus, le bâtiment original du
couvent.*

The entrance atrium area: its vaulted space
serves as a transition to Botta's powerfully
modern library. The arcades here were existing
elements of the Convent's portico.
 *Die Eingangshalle mit Kreuzgewölben –
ursprünglich Teil des Säulengangs des Klosters –
bildet den Übergang vom Altbau zu Bottas kraftvoll modernem Bibliotheksgebäude.*
 *L'atrium d'entrée dont l'espace voûté sert
de transition à la bibliothèque puissamment
moderne de Botta. Les arcades appartiennent
à l'ancien bâtiment du couvent.*

A notch-like form cuts through the painted white-finish brick to reveal the underlying concrete. The same notch is visible in the left wall below. The concrete walls and coffers, together with a strong sense of axial symmetry, give the reading room a power that belies its relatively small size.

Eine Art hammerförmiger Einschnitt in der weißgetünchten Backsteinwand legt den darunterliegenden Beton frei. Die gleiche Kerbe ist unten an der linken Wand zu sehen. Die Betonwände und -kassetten verleihen dem Lesesaal im Verbund mit seiner dominanten Axialsymmetrie eine Ausdruckskraft, die in keinem Verhältnis zu seinen relativ kleinen Dimensionen steht.

La forme à encoche découpée dans la brique peinte en blanc révèle le béton du mur. La même découpe s'entrevoit sur le mur gauche du dessous. Les murs, le plafond à caissons en béton et la symétrie axiale appuyée confèrent à cette salle de lecture une réelle puissance malgré ses dimensions relativement réduites.

Office Building "Ransila 1"
Lugano, Switzerland, 1981–1985

Located in central Lugano, 500 meters from the lake, this building is set on a corner. A reinforced concrete structure, it is faced in red brick. As the architect says, "I use brick as a facing material because it never appears to hold the structure up, but instead it seems to be held up by the structure underneath." The site is 850 square meters for a net floor area of 4,000 square meters. One unusual feature of the building is Mario Botta's decision to place a single tree at its highest point. He continues, "I fell in love with a tree that reverses the usual rules. It represents nature *on* architecture. There is a tower in Lucca in Italy that has a tree at its highest point. The tree grew there accidentally, but over the centuries, it became magnificent. This is a very lively idea that seems quite different from our usual concept of modernity. There is a question of the relationship of architecture to the sky, which I feel is just as important as its relationship to the ground."

Das Büro- und Geschäftshaus »Ransila 1« in Lugano, dessen Stockwerke zu beiden Seiten des Eckturms treppenartig anzusteigen scheinen, ist mit roten Ziegelsteinen verkleidet. Der Architekt erläutert dazu: »Ich verwende Ziegelsteine als Fassadenmaterial, weil sie nie so aussehen, als würden sie die Konstruktion stützen, sondern vielmehr, als würden sie von der darunterliegenden Konstruktion getragen.« Das Grundstück umfaßt 850 m²; das Gebäude verfügt über eine Gesamtfläche von 4 000 m². Ein ungewöhnliches Gestaltungselement ist der einzelne Baum, den Mario Botta auf die höchste Stelle des Bürohauses pflanzen ließ. Wie er selbst sagt, »verliebte er sich« in einen Baum, »der die üblichen Regeln umkehrt. Er repräsentiert die Natur *auf* einem Werk der Architektur. In der Stadt Lucca in Italien gibt es einen alten Turm, auf dem ein Baum wächst, der aus einem zufällig dort hingewehten Samen entstand ... Das ist eine sehr lebendige Entwurfsidee, die sich von unserem üblichen Konzept der Moderne ziemlich deutlich unterscheidet. Ich halte die Frage nach der Beziehung von Gebäuden zum Himmel für ebenso wichtig wie deren Beziehung zum Boden, auf dem sie stehen.«

Situé dans le centre de Lugano, à 500 m du lac, cet immeuble occupe une parcelle d'angle. En béton armé, il est recouvert de brique rouge. « J'utilise la brique en parement parce qu'elle ne donne jamais l'impression de soutenir la structure, mais plutôt d'être soutenue par elle. » Le terrain mesure 850 m² et le bâtiment 4 000. Un des détails curieux de ce bâtiment est l'arbre solitaire que l'architecte a planté à son sommet. Comme il l'explique : « Je suis tombé amoureux de l'idée d'un arbre qui inverse les règles habituelles. Il représente la nature *sur* l'architecture. Cette idée de vie est très différente des concepts que nous rattachons habituellement à la modernité. C'est un problème de relation de l'architecture avec le ciel, qui à mon avis, est aussi importante que celle qu'elle entretient avec le sol. »

The "Ransila 1" Building, with its solitary tree on the roof, and its strong, stepped-notch openings, creates a sense of place, and of transition from one street to another. Despite the building's mass, the brick cladding gives a degree of warmth to the design.

Das Büro- und Geschäftshaus »Ransila 1« mit dem einzelnen Baum auf dem Dach und seinen zu beiden Seiten des Treppenturms abgetreppten Fensterreihen wirkt »ortsbildend«, und zwar als Ort des Übergangs zwischen den beiden Straßen, deren eine Ecke es füllt. Trotz seiner Größe vermittelt es aufgrund seiner Ziegelsteinfassade den Eindruck von Wärme.

L'immeuble « Ransila 1 », son arbre solitaire sur le toit et ses puissantes découpes créent un sens du lieu, tout en aménageant une transition entre les rues. Le parement en brique des façades humanise la masse assez imposante de l'immeuble.

As seen in its urban environment, the "Ransila 1"
Building stands out from neighboring buildings
without disfiguring the rhythm of the corner in
any way. Below right: a section, and plans of the
ground, middle and top floors.

   In dem städtischen Kontext hebt sich das
»Ransila-1«-Gebäude von seinen Nachbarbauten
ab, ohne den Rhythmus der Platzbebauung zu
stören. Unten rechts ein Querschnitt sowie
Grundrisse des Erdgeschosses sowie des zweiten
und obersten Geschosses.

   Dans son environnement urbain, le « Ransila 1 » se détache des constructions voisines sans
pour autant rompre le rythme de l'angle de rue.
En bas à droite, coupe, plan au sol, plan d'étage
intermédiaire et du dernier niveau.

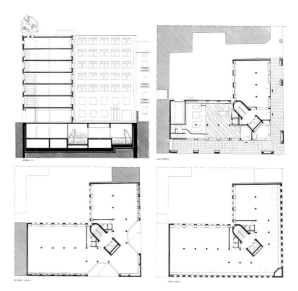

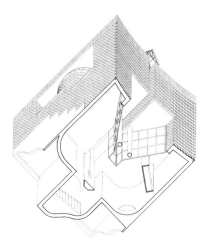

Single Family House
Morbio Superiore, Ticino, Switzerland, 1982–1983

Using untreated cement blocks on the exterior, which are simply painted white inside and complemented with black slate floors, Mario Botta affirms a style that is not necessary brutal, but which certainly aspires to a certain geometric simplicity in this 300 square meter house. "Like a squirrel," the architect explains, "I wanted to hollow out the form inside and cut the house out of the hill with a knife so to speak, using only the floor at the top as an entrance. The slightly curved façade on the downhill side, on the other hand, belongs more to the landscape than to the house itself. For this reason, it is a concave façade which traps light and makes it resonate at different times of the day." He also says, "Since it is partially dug out of the mountain, the house in Morbio has something of a cave, while at the same time it opens out to the sky. Although you remain in your home, you retain some relationship to the outside world."

Mit diesem Gebäude aus Zementstein – außen unbehandelt, innen schlicht weiß gestrichen und mit schwarzen Schieferböden ausgelegt – bekennt sich Botta zu einem Stil, der nicht zwingend »brutal« ist, der aber ganz offensichtlich auf 300 m² Wohnfläche eine überschaubare, schlichte Geometrie umzusetzen sucht. »Wie ein Eichhörnchen wollte ich die Gebäudeform von innen aushöhlen«, sagt Botta, »das Haus sozusagen mit einem Meißel aus dem Hügel hauen und nur das oberste Geschoß als Eingangsebene nutzen. Die leicht geschwungene Fassade zum Abhang ist mehr ein Teil der Landschaft als des Hauses selbst. Aus diesem Grund handelt es sich um eine konkave Fläche, die das Licht einfängt und zu unterschiedlichen Tageszeiten reflektiert.« An anderer Stelle bemerkt er: »Da es zum Teil in den Berg eingegraben ist, ähnelt das Haus in Morbio einer Höhle, die sich gleichzeitig zum Himmel öffnet. Obwohl man in seinem Haus bleibt, behält man den Bezug zur Außenwelt.«

À partir de blocs de ciment brut pour l'extérieur, simplement peints en blanc sur leur face intérieure, et d'un sol en ardoise noire, Mario Botta affirme un style qui, s'il n'est pas vraiment brutal, tend à affirmer la pureté géométrique de cette maison familiale de 300 m². « Tel un écureuil », commente-t-il, « je voulais creuser la forme de l'intérieur et tailler la maison dans la colline, au couteau pour ainsi dire, en implantant l'entrée au niveau supérieur. La façade légèrement incurvée côté pente appartient plus au paysage qu'à la maison elle-même. Concave, elle piège la lumière qui multiplie ses aspects selon les heures du jour. » « Comme elle est en partie creusée dans la montagne, cette maison familiale possède quelques caractéristiques de la caverne, tout en s'ouvrant en même temps vers le ciel. Même en restant chez vous, vous conservez ainsi une sorte de relation avec le monde extérieur », ajoute l'architecte.

Above, an axonometric drawing shows the house as seen from below. To the right a detail shows the unusual 45° angle at which alternating bands of construction block are laid. Set on its own, the house stands out starkly against the countryside (p. 60). The notch that appears in the façade also occurs within the house (p. 61), underlining its basic symmetry.

Die Axonometrie zeigt das Haus in Untersicht. Rechts ein Detail der im ungewöhnlichen Winkel von 45° gemauerten Ziegelsteinbänder im Wechsel mit glatt gemauerten. Das frei stehende Haus bildet einen starken Kontrast zur Landschaft (S. 60), seine tief eingeschnittene Fassadenöffnung durchbricht die konkave Fläche der Hauptfront. Die gleiche Art Einschnitt im Innern des Hauses (S. 61) unterstreicht dessen grundlegende, durchgängige Symmetrie.

Ci-dessus, représentation axonométrique de la maison vue par dessous. À droite, détail montrant le montage inhabituel à 45° des parpaings en bandeaux alternés. Isolée, la maison se détache fortement de son paysage (p. 60). La surface concave de la façade principale est marquée par une large ouverture en encoche. Le même type de découpe se retrouve à l'intérieur (p. 61).

To the left, the dining area. The concave surface
of the house (above) catches the light and, accor-
ding to the angle, makes it appear more or less
complex. To the right, the balcony set back into
the central opening in the façade.

*Links die Eßecke. In Abhängigkeit vom
Sonnenlauf und der sich daraus ergebenden
Schattenbildung wirkt die konkave Fassade des
Hauses (oben) tagsüber mehr oder weniger stark
gemustert. Rechts die in das Hausinnere zurück-
tretende Balkonterrasse.*

À gauche, le coin salle à manger. Sur cette
page, la façade concave de la maison prend la
lumière, qui la fait paraître plus ou moins complexe selon l'angle du soleil. À droite, le balcon
aménagé dans l'ouverture centrale de la façade.

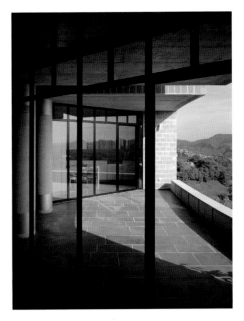

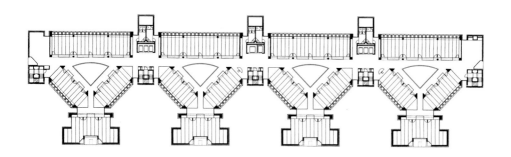

Gottardo Bank
Lugano, Switzerland, 1982–1988

Divided into four blocks separated by stair towers, this 14,000 square meter building is an imposing presence, contrary to much contemporary bank architecture. As Mario Botta says "Cities are places for exchanging, meeting, trading. A bank is part of this process. Recent trends have tended on the contrary to see banks merely as a collection of administrative units: unwilling or unable to make their mark on the urban context. In fact, many bank buildings have used a neutral, international design on generally tried and accepted lines. Local circumstances, the historical and geographical context, and the particular characteristics of the site itself were often ignored. My design for the Gottardo Bank offices tries to take the opposite approach, by using the existing urban setting as the starting point for the design." The basic floor plan of the four towers along the Viale Franscini is similar to that of the Library of the Capuchin Convent.

Das Gebäude der Banca del Gottardo besteht aus vier Teilen, die durch Treppenhäuser miteinander verbunden sind und eine Gesamtfläche von 14 000 m² einnehmen. Anders als manche zeitgenössische Bankgebäude dominiert dieser Komplex seine Umgebung. Botta meint dazu: »Städte sind Orte des Austauschs, der Begegnung, des Handels. Eine Bank ist Teil dieser Prozesse. In jüngster Zeit hat man dazu tendiert, Banken nur als Ansammlung administrativer Einheiten zu verstehen, die entweder nicht willens oder nicht in der Lage sind, ihrem jeweiligen städtischen Kontext ihren eigenen Stempel aufzudrücken. Tatsächlich haben viele Banken für ihre Gebäude einen neutralen, internationalen Stil nach allgemein bewährtem und akzeptiertem Rezept gewählt. Lokale Gegebenheiten, der historische und geographische Kontext und die Besonderheiten des Baugrundstücks selbst wurden häufig ignoriert. Beim Entwurf des Gotthard-Bankgebäudes verfolgte ich den entgegengesetzten Ansatz, indem ich den Bestand als Ausgangspunkt nutzte.«

Divisé en quatre blocs séparés par des cages d'escalier, cet immeuble de 14 000 m² impose sa présence, à la différence de beaucoup d'exemples contemporains d'architecture bancaire. Comme le précise Mario Botta : « Les villes sont des lieux d'échange, de rencontre, de commerce. Une banque fait partie de ce schéma. Les tendances récentes veulent au contraire que les banques soient des ensembles d'unités administratives, incapables ou ne souhaitant pas marquer le contexte urbain. En fait, de nombreux immeubles de banques se tournent vers un style international neutre et des solutions éprouvées et acceptées. Les circonstances locales, le contexte historique et géographique, et les caractéristiques particulières du terrain sont souvent ignorées. Mon projet pour les bureaux de la banque du Gotthard essaye de privilégier l'approche opposée, en prenant pour point de départ le cadre urbain. » Le plan au sol des quatre tours le long de la Viale Franscini est similaire à celui de la bibliothèque du couvent des Capucins.

The strong notched blocks that form the four main volumes of the bank stand out against the skyline of Lugano. The basic, modular floor plan recalls that of the Morbio Inferiore Middle School in a more articulated or martial configuration.

Die »tief eingekerbten« vier Gebäudeblöcke der Bank bilden in der Skyline von Lugano einen starken Akzent. Der modulare Aufbau erinnert an den der Realschule in Morbio Inferiore, allerdings ist er hier stärker gegliedert und wuchtiger.

Des blocs profondément découpés constituent les quatre volumes principaux de la banque. Le plan au sol, modulaire, rappelle celui de l'école primaire de Morbio Inferiore d'une façon plus articulée, voire martiale.

The powerful, almost military appearance of the
four main volumes reinforces the alignment of
the buildings along the street, but also stands
apart because of the singularity of the façades
themselves.

Die vier mächtigen, fast festungsartigen
Gebäudevolumen mit ihrer ungewöhnlichen
Fassadengestaltung markieren die Baulinie an
der Straßenfront.

L'aspect puissant, presque militaire, des
quatre volumes principaux renforce l'effet
d'alignement le long de la rue, mais les distingue
néanmoins de leur environnement par leur
singularité.

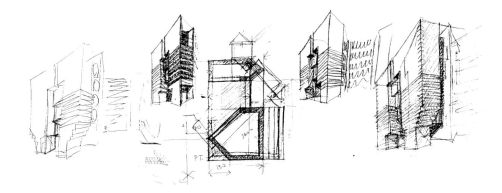

*Above, personal sketches by Mario Botta show
the presence of the volumes of the bank as seen
notably from the street. Below, the banded stone
finish, a typical element of Botta's style, here runs
through two powerful columns that guard the
entrance to the bank.*

*Oben: Mario Bottas Skizzen zeigen Straßen-
ansichten der vier Hauptvolumen. Die für Botta
typischen Wandverkleidungen aus verschiedenfar-
bigen Steinbändern werden auch von den beiden
Säulen aufgenommen, die den Eingang zur
Schalterhalle »bewachen« (unten).*

*En haut, croquis de Mario Botta illustrant la
forte présence des volumes de la banque, en particulier vus de la rue. Ci-dessous, les bandeaux de
pierre, typiques du style de Botta, courent sur les
deux puissantes colonnes qui gardent l'entrée de
la banque.*

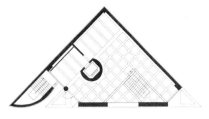

Watari-um Contemporary Art Gallery
Tokyo, Japan, 1985–1990

Set on a 157 square meter triangular lot, this art gallery stands out from its environment. The inlaid stone effect of the façade and its massive solidity signal its atypical design in a city that is entirely given over to ephemeral architecture. In a letter to his client written in 1990, the architect stated, "In the Babel of urban languages that changes daily, I wanted to test the 'durability' of a strong, primary image, an architecture generated by the building's own inner logic, its geometry and the effects of light. My hope is, dear 'difficult' Mrs. Watari, that 'our' Watari-um will live for centuries, like the Romanesque buildings." Although the architect's words are tinged with a certain irony here, the building does assume a stance of durability against the ephemeral nature of Tokyo. The structure features a basement bookstore, a double-height exhibition area on the first floor, and a small apartment on the top level, the whole set into a net floor area of 627 square meters.

Die Galerie für zeitgenössische Kunst fand Platz auf einer dreieckigen Fläche von 157 m². Der Inkrustationseffekt der Steinfassade und der massiv und solide wirkende Baukörper setzen ein untypisches Architektursignal in einer Stadt, die fast ausschließlich aus Leichtbauten besteht. In einem Brief an seine Bauherrin schrieb der Architekt im Jahr 1990 mit einer gewissen Ironie: »Im Babel der täglich wechselnden städtischen Formensprachen wollte ich die ›Haltbarkeit‹ eines starken elementaren Erscheinungsbilds testen, einen Architekturstil, der sich aus der inneren Logik des Bauwerks ergibt, aus seiner Geometrie und seinen Lichtwirkungen. Ich hoffe, liebe ›schwierige‹ Mrs. Watari, daß ›unser‹ Watari-um Jahrhunderte überdauern wird – genau wie die Bauten der Romanik.« Die Galerie beherbergt einen Buchladen im Untergeschoß, einen Ausstellungsbereich von doppelter Geschoßhöhe im Erdgeschoß und eine kleine Wohnung auf der oberen Ebene – und alle zusammen umfassen nur 627 m².

Sur une parcelle triangulaire de 157 m², cette galerie d'art contemporain se détache de son environnement. L'effet de marqueterie de pierre de la façade et la solidité de son apparence massive sont atypiques dans une ville entièrement vouée à l'architecture éphémère. Dans une lettre à sa cliente rédigée en 1990, l'architecte écrivait : « Dans cette Babel de langages urbanistiques qui se modifient chaque jour, je voulais tester la ‹ durabilité › d'une image forte et primaire, d'une architecture générée par la propre logique intérieure du bâtiment, la géométrie et les effets de la lumière. Mon espoir, chère et ‹ difficile › Mrs. Watari est que ‹ notre › Watari-um vivra des siècles, comme les constructions romanes. » Même si l'architecte ne manque pas d'une certaine ironie, ce petit bâtiment affirme une volonté de durée face à la nature éphémère de la majorité de l'architecture de la capitale japonaise. Il comprend une librairie en sous-sol, un espace d'exposition à double hauteur au rez-de-chaussée et un petit appartement en étage, le tout sur 627 m².

An axonometric drawing and a floor plan highlight the basic simplicity of the triangular design. The Watari-um Gallery has a banded, centrally notched façade, with a cylindrical volume set on the roof. In the extremely dense and heterogeneous urban environment of Tokyo, the Gallery stands out (pp. 70/71; to the left) because of its unusually powerful symmetry and stone façades.

Grundriß und axonometrische Darstellung machen deutlich, wie schlicht der Entwurf ist, der dem Gebäude zugrunde liegt. Die Galerie Watari-um weist eine Fassade mit »Streifenmuster« und hammerförmigem Einschnitt (Eingang) auf (rechts); sie wird von einem zylinderförmigen Element bekrönt. Obwohl die Galerie (S. 70/71; Mitte links unten) inmitten der Stadt Tokio steht, hebt sie sich aufgrund ihrer ungewöhnlich kraftvollen Symmetrie und quergestreiften Steinfassaden von ihrer Umgebung ab.

Plan au sol et vue axonométrique qui soulignent la simplicité basique du plan en triangle. La galerie Watari-um possède une façade à bandeaux et à découpe, surmontée ici d'une colonne cylindrique sur le toit. La galerie (pp. 70/71; à gauche) ressort de l'environnement urbain extrêmement dense et hétérogène de Tokyo par sa symétrie et ses façades de pierre.

Seen from street level, the Watari-um Gallery
does not fundamentally contradict any of its
architectural environment, but it does introduce
an element of rigor and power that was otherwise
lacking – rigor and power that are also visible in
the interior view to the left.

Von der Straße aus gesehen, bildet die Galerie Watari-um keinen grundlegenden Widerspruch zu ihrer gebauten Umwelt, sie vermittelt
jedoch eine Strenge und Kraft, die den Nachbarbauten fehlt und die auch innen zu spüren sind
(links).

Vue du niveau de la rue, la galerie ne con-
tredit pas fondamentalement son environnement
architectural, mais introduit un élément de ri-
gueur et de force également sensible à l'intérieur
(à gauche).

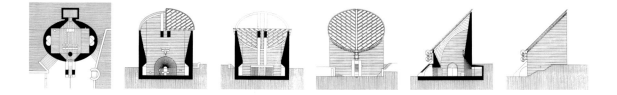

Church of Saint John the Baptist

Mogno, Valle Maggia, Ticino, Switzerland, 1986/92–1998

Following a catastrophic double avalanche, which swept away most of the village of Mogno in a remote valley of southern Switzerland in 1986, the mayor of the town, Giovan Luigi Dazio, called on Mario Botta to design a church to replace the seventeenth-century edifice that had stood there. Botta's response for the 178 square meter site was an unusual oval plan, which resembles a truncated cylinder in elevation. The design drew substantial criticism, which delayed the construction and coincidentally led to Botta receiving another commission for a chapel on the Monte Tamaro. Clad in white Peccia marble and Riveo gray granite, both of which are locally mined, the completed chapel stands as a defiant symbol of solidity, affirmed in its opposition to the strength of nature. The alternating bands of white and gray, together with the density of the stone, evoke the Romanesque architecture of which Botta is admittedly quite fond, while the strict use of geometry makes it clear that this is no pastiche.

Im Jahr 1986 ging im südschweizerischen Maggia-Tal eine zweifache Felslawine nieder und zerstörte das Dorf Mogno weitgehend. Bürgermeister Giovan Luigi Dazio erteilte Mario Botta den Auftrag, die zerstörte Kirche des 17. Jahrhunderts durch einen Neubau zu ersetzen. Botta präsentierte einen ungewöhnlichen Entwurf für das 178 m² große Grundstück: einen ovalen Baukörper, der von außen wie ein abgeschrägter Zylinder wirkt. Er stieß damit auf erhebliche Kritik, was die Durchführung des Baus verzögerte, dem Architekten aber auch einen weiteren Auftrag zum Bau einer Kapelle auf dem Monte Tamaro einbrachte. Die Dorfkirche, Johannes dem Täufer geweiht (San Giovanni Battista), ist mit weißem Peccia-Marmor und grauem Riveo-Granit aus nahe gelegenen Steinbrüchen verkleidet und steht als trutziges Symbol für Widerstandsfähigkeit gegenüber den Kräften der Natur. Die Fassadenbänder und die Massivität des Baumaterials lassen an romanische Bauten denken, die Botta sehr schätzt, während der streng geometrische Aufbau der Kirche samt Zylinderstumpf deutlich macht, daß es sich hier keineswegs um ein »Imitat« handelt.

À la suite de la catastrophique double avalanche qui a rayé de la carte la plus grande partie du village de Mogno dans une lointaine vallée de la Suisse méridionale en 1986, le maire, Giovan Luigi Dazio, fit appel à Mario Botta pour dessiner l'église destinée à remplacer l'édifice du XVIIᵉ siècle qui avait été détruit. La proposition de Botta pour ce terrain de 178 m² prit la forme d'un curieux plan ovale faisant penser en élévation à un cylindre tronqué. Le projet provoqua une controverse, qui retarda la construction mais rapporta à l'architecte la commande d'une autre chapelle sur le Monte Tamaro. Recouverte de marbre de Peccia et de granit gris de Riveo l'église Saint-Jean-Baptiste est un symbole de solidité et un défi jeté à la puissance de la nature. Les bandeaux alternés gris et blancs et la densité de la pierre évoquent l'architecture romane, qu'apprécie particulièrement Botta, mais le strict recours à la géométrie écarte toute idée de pastiche.

The Church of Saint John the Baptist has an oval plan, which is resolved into a tilted, circular skylight. Clad in alternating bands of white marble and gray granite, the church is approached via a white marble square (p. 76), also designed by Botta. Inside, the same gray and white banded design lends itself to a Romanesque feeling of solidity and timelessness (p. 77).

Der Hauptraum der Kirche ist ein ovaler, oben abgeschrägter Zylinderstumpf. Die steil geneigte Dachfläche bildet zugleich das Oberlicht. Der Kirchenbau ist mit weißem Marmor und grauem Granit verkleidet (S. 76) und über einen weißen Marmorplatz erreichbar, den ebenfalls Botta gestaltete. Im Innern (S. 77) trägt das gleiche grau-weiße »Streifenmuster« zum Eindruck von Solidität und Zeitlosigkeit bei.

L'église Saint-Jean-Baptiste est construite sur un plan en ovale, et surmontée d'un toit-verrière circulaire incliné. Recouverte de bandeaux alternés de granit gris et de marbre blanc, l'église donne sur une place de marbre blanc (p. 76), également dessinée par Botta. À l'intérieur (p. 77), le même motif alterné donne un sentiment quasi roman de solidité et d'intemporalité.

As seen from the pedestrian approach path, a white marble fountain designed by Mario Botta marks the entrance to the area of the church. To the right, the very large oculus of the church brings direct sunlight down to the floor at certain hours, and changes dramatically with the passage of clouds, for example.

Neben der Einfahrt zum Kirchplatz hat Botta einen weißen Mamorbrunnen (eigener Entwurf) plaziert. Der große oculus (rechts) sorgt je nach Wetterlage für wechselnde Lichtstimmungen im Raum und läßt zu bestimmten Tageszeiten direktes Sonnenlicht bis auf den Fußboden fallen.

Au bord de l'allée piétonnière qui y conduit, une fontaine de marbre blanc dessinée par Mario Botta marque l'entrée de l'enceinte de l'église. À droite, la très large verrière laisse pénétrer un éclairage direct qui frappe le sol à certaines heures, et se modifie spectaculairement, au passage des nuages par exemple.

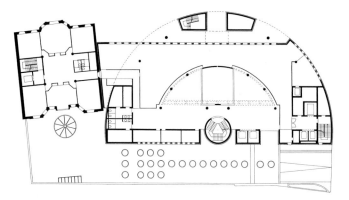

Union Bank of Switzerland
Basel, Switzerland, 1986–1995

Located at the corner of St-Jakobs-Strasse on the Aeschengraben, a large urban square in the heart of Basel, the UBS building assumes a symbolic importance in perfect harmony with its architecture. A semicircular form with a radius of 26 meters dominates the plan of this building, which has a gross floor area of 8,700 square meters, and a height above street level of 28 meters. Designed with a structure of reinforced concrete pillars, walls, and floor slabs, the UBS building is clad in bands of sea-green granite and Viscount white marble. Porphyry is used for external paving, while natural stone slabs and glossy Cambrian granite alternate for the interior floors of the public areas. Massive, and unashamed of its imposing presence, Botta's design does reflect the central place of banking in the Swiss economy, but those who are fond of his smaller work may not necessarily adhere to this shift of scale.

Das Gebäude der »Schweizerischen Bankgesellschaft« befindet sich an der Ecke Aeschengraben / St.-Jakobs-Straße an einem großen Platz im Herzen der Stadt Basel. Seine Funktion und symbolische Bedeutung stehen in vollkommenem Einklang mit seiner architektonischen Gestaltung. Ein halbrundes Volumen mit einem Durchmesser von 26 m ist das beherrschende Element. Das Gebäude hat eine Bruttogeschoßfläche von 8 700 m² und erhebt sich 28 m über dem Straßenniveau. Die Stahlbetonkonstruktion besteht aus Stützpfeilern sowie Wand- und Bodenplatten, die Fassadenverkleidung aus meergrünen Granit- und weißen Marmorbändern. Porphyrsteine wurden im Außenbereich zur Pflasterung verwendet, während für die Fußböden der öffentlich zugänglichen Räumlichkeiten Natursteinplatten und polierter walisischer Granit gewählt wurden. Bottas Bankgebäude behauptet sich selbstbewußt an seinem Platz und spiegelt die zentrale Rolle des Bankwesens in der Schweizer Wirtschaft. Diejenigen, die Bottas kleinere Bauten schätzen, werden jedoch möglicherweise Schwierigkeiten haben, diesen Wechsel der Größenverhältnisse zu akzeptieren.

À l'angle de la St-Jakobs-Strasse et l'Aeschengraben, une vaste place du centre de Bâle, l'immeuble de l'UBS (Union des Banques Suisses) affirme son importance symbolique en parfaite harmonie avec son architecture. Une forme semi-circulaire de 26 m de rayon domine le plan de cet immeuble de 8 700 m² et de 28 m de haut. Recouvert de bandeaux alternés de granit vert et de marbre blanc Viscount, il possède une structure à piliers de béton armé, des murs et des sols en dalles de béton. Le porphyre a été retenu pour les sols extérieurs, et les dalles de pierre et de granit gallois poli alternent au sol des espaces publics intérieurs. Massif et sans complexe par rapport à sa massive présence, le projet de Botta reflète le rôle central de la banque dans l'économie suisse. Tous ceux qui apprécient ses œuvres de plus petites dimensions, n'adhèrent pas forcément à cette amplification d'échelle.

A side view of the main semicircular volume gives the impression of an almost blank façade. Further openings mark the entrance, around the corner. Alternating bands of granite and marble together with the strong geometric form of the bank clearly mark this as a Mario Botta building.

Die Seitenansicht des halbrunden Hauptbaukörpers vermittelt den Eindruck, als sei die Fassade nahezu geschlossen. Aufgrund der Fassadenbänder aus abwechselnd weißem Marmor und meergrünem Granit ist dieses Bankgebäude eindeutig als Werk Mario Bottas zu erkennen.

La vue latérale du volume principal en demi-cercle donne l'impression d'une façade presque aveugle. Des ouvertures signalent l'entrée implantée dans l'angle. Les bandeaux alternés de granit et de marbre et la puissante et austère géométrie appartiennent au vocabulaire traditionnel de Botta.

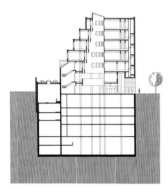

Stepped up to the rear, as seen in a section (left), the building's fundamental solidity is marked by generous openings such as the semicircular height of the entrance lobby area (below, looking up).

Auf der Rückseite ist das Gebäude abgetreppt (links). Es wirkt zwar massiv, besitzt aber großzügige Öffnungen und Räume, wie etwa die halbkreisförmige, bis auf Dachhöhe reichende Eingangshalle (unten, Blick nach oben).

Découpée en escalier, comme le montre la coupe de gauche, la masse du bâtiment est ponctuée de généreuses ouvertures comme la verrière semi-circulaire de l'atrium d'entrée (ci-dessous, vers le haut).

Mario Botta's own sketches tend to give a very accurate view of the completed buildings. As seen here from the square, the bank appears to be entirely circular, its stepped, notched openings almost recalling the neighboring roof lines.

Vom Platz aus gesehen wirkt das Bankgebäude wie ein Rundbau. Der für Botta typische »Hammer« bildet hier nicht den Einschnitt in der Fassade, sondern tritt durch die zu beiden Seiten treppenartig ansteigenden Fassadenrücksprünge massiv hervor.

Les premiers croquis de Mario Botta fournissent une vision très précise des bâtiments achevés. Vue de la place, la banque semble totalement ronde, ses ouvertures en escalier rappelant presque la ligne des toits du voisinage.

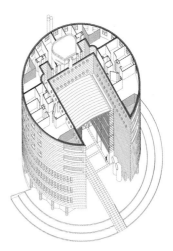

Residences, Offices and Shops
Lugano-Paradiso, Switzerland, 1986–1992

This large (4,300 square meter) red brick building, known as the "Centro Cinque Continenti" (Center of Five Continents), is quite visible from the main road that leads out of Lugano toward the Paradiso area and along the banks of the lake to Chiasso. Its construction material, as well as its bold form, clearly signal that this is a building by Mario Botta. A green metalwork canopy stands high above the entrance area, which is treated with large areas of glass blocks. The basic floor plan of the building is circular, with a large three-sided rectilinear notch carved out of the entrance zone. The large curved façade that faces away from the lake is defined by three bands of small rectangular windows, which give way to three rows of larger, square windows above.

Das große rote Backsteingebäude (4 300 m² Nutzfläche) trägt die Bezeichnung »Centro Cinque Continenti« (Zentrum der fünf Kontinente) und ist von der Hauptausfallstraße her sichtbar, die von Lugano nach Paradiso und dann am Ufer des Sees entlang in Richtung Chiasso führt. Sowohl die Baumaterialien als auch die gewagte Form signalisieren deutlich, daß es sich um ein Bauwerk Mario Bottas handelt. Ein grünes Metallvordach schwebt hoch über dem Eingang zu dem im Grundriß kreisrunden Gebäude; den Eingangsbereich selbst jedoch bildet eine große rechtwinklige Einbuchtung, die auf ihren drei Begrenzungsseiten Flächen aus Glasbausteinen aufweist. Drei horizontal verlaufende Fensterbänder aus kleinen rechteckigen Öffnungen, über denen sich wiederum drei Reihen größerer quadratischer Fenster erheben, prägen die mächtige, gerundete Fassade auf der vom See abgewandten Seite.

Ce vaste bâtiment de brique rouge (4 300 m²), appelé le « Centro Cinque Continenti » (Centre de cinq continents) est visible de l'axe routier qui mène de Lugano au quartier de Paradiso le long des rives du lac en allant vers Chiasso. Ses matériaux de construction et sa forme audacieuse signalent clairement qu'il s'agit d'une œuvre de Mario Botta. Un dais de métal vert domine de haut une entrée traitée en grands panneaux de verre. Le plan au sol est de forme circulaire, interrompu par une grande indentation rectiligne sur trois côtés, pratiquée dans la zone d'entrée. L'importante façade incurvée qui est détournée du lac est rythmée par trois bandeaux de petites fenêtres rectangulaires, auxquels succèdent trois rangées de grandes baies carrées.

The plan of the Center is entirely circular, as can be seen in the axonometric drawing above. The entrance area with its generous canopy cuts a rectangular notch into the basic cylinder. The considerable height of the entrance makes the building visibly open.

Im Plan ist das Gebäude kreisförmig (s. Axonometrie). Eine rechteckige Hohlform schneidet in den Gebäudezylinder hinein. Sie bildet den Hauptzugangsbereich mit großem Vordach, der zugleich Innenhof ist (rechts).

Le plan de l'immeuble est entièrement circulaire, comme le montre le dessin axonométrique ci-dessus. L'aire d'entrée surmontée d'un énorme auvent découpe une entaille rectangulaire dans ce cylindre. La hauteur considérable de l'entrée donne l'impression que le bâtiment est très ouvert.

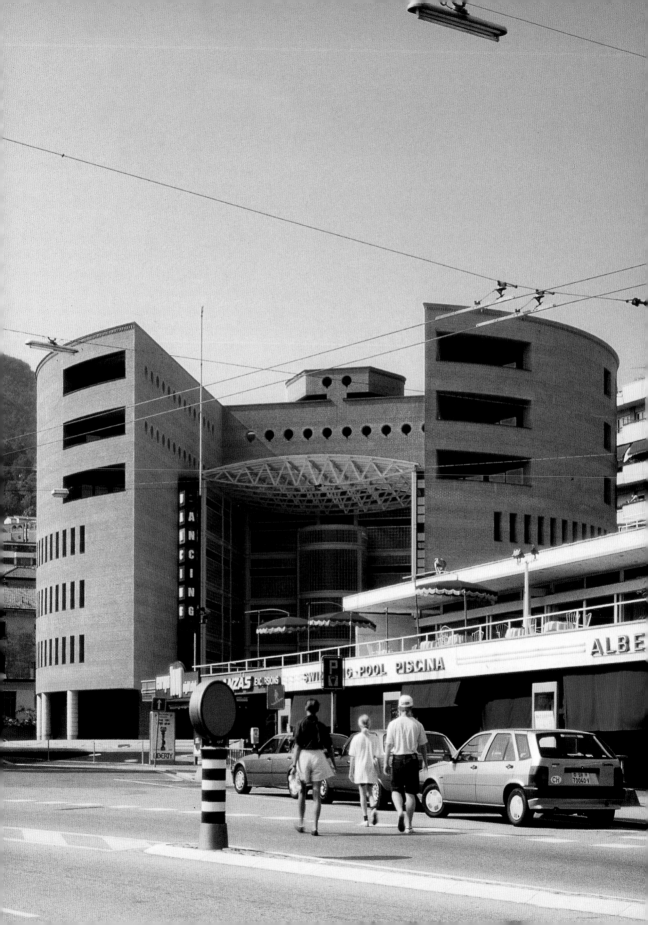

The low angle of this image emphasizes the almost anthropomorphic aspect of the building, its semicircular volumes resembling open arms. Balconies and high rectangular windows mark the exterior façade.

Aus dem sehr niedrigen Blickwinkel des Fotografen hat der Bau fast etwas Anthropomorphes: die nach vorne greifenden halbkreisförmigen Gebäudeteile wirken wie ausgebreitete Arme. Balkone sowie hohe schmale oder große breite Fensteröffnungen akzentuieren die Fassade.

Cette photographie en contre-plongée fait ressortir le caractère presque anthropomorphique du bâtiment, dont les volumes semi-circulaires font penser à deux bras ouverts. La façade extérieure est animée par de hautes fenêtres rectangulaires et des balcons.

The green metalwork gives an unexpected degree of freshness to the entrance area. Within the central, circular volume, a partially open stairway is highlighted against a glass-block background.

Die grüngestrichenen, glasgedeckten Fachwerkträger des Vordachs vermitteln den Eindruck von Frische im Eingangsbereich. Ein teilweise offenes Treppenhaus ist in einem Zylinder aus Glasbausteinen untergebracht.

Les éléments métalliques peints en vert donnent une fraîcheur inattendue à l'aire de l'entrée. À l'intérieur du volume cylindrique central, l'escalier se détache en contre-jour sur la paroi en pavés de verre de la cage d'escalier en partie ouverte.

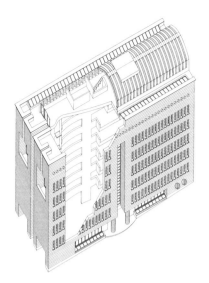

Bruxelles Lambert Bank
Geneva, Switzerland, 1987–1996

Another large bank building, perhaps more austere than others designed by Botta, the Bruxelles Lambert Bank features two distinct tower-like forms on its northern façade. With a site area of 1,160 square meters, the structure has a floor area of 4,500 square meters. It is 28 meters high, with overall measurements of 41 x 16 meters. Mario Botta recalls, "This project was the outcome of a competition, and the building limits, width, depth and height were all set out in detail in the master plan for the area. Given these constraints, the design attempts to highlight a number of points of interest in relation to the city. The short front on the plaza is treated as two towers whose monumental scale characterizes the free public space." Clad in Pietra Dorata natural stone, the building is designed as a notched rectangle, with sharp vertical indentations on three sides. The longer sides feature five rows of high vertical windows on either side of the central notch.

Vielleicht etwas strenger, reduzierter gestaltet als seine anderen Entwürfe für Banken, präsentiert sich Bottas Neubau der Bank Bruxelles Lambert. Das Grundstück umfaßt 1 160 m², das Gebäude mit seinen beiden turmartigen, nach Norden gerichteten Baukörpern verfügt über eine Gesamtfläche von 4 500 m², eine Höhe von 28 m und mißt im Plan 41 x 16 m. »Der Bau ist das Ergebnis eines Wettbewerbs«, so Botta, »und die Baulinien – Breite, Höhe und Tiefe des Neubaus – waren im Generalplan für das Bebauungsgebiet detailliert festgelegt. Diese Einschränkungen berücksichtigend, versucht der Entwurf, eine Reihe von Bezugspunkten zum Stadtbild zu betonen. Zwei Türme bilden die knapp bemessene Platzfront, deren Monumentalität den freien öffentlichen Raum prägt.« Der Neubau ist mit Natursteinen (pietra dorata) verkleidet und stellt im wesentlichen einen eingekerbten Rechteckblock dar: Von der Südseite abgesehen sind die Fassaden mit vertikalen Einschnitten versehen; auf den Längsseiten sind diese in fünf Reihen hochrechteckiger Fenster angeordnet, die einen zentralen großen Einschnitt flankieren.

Nouvel immeuble bancaire, peut-être plus austère encore que d'autres dessinés par Botta, la banque Bruxelles Lambert se signale par les deux tours de sa façade nord. Pour un terrain de 1 160 m² et une surface utile de 4 500 m², le bâtiment mesure 41 x 16 m sur 28 m de haut. Mario Botta à déclaré à son sujet : « Ce projet est le résultat d'un concours, et les dimensions – largeur, hauteur et profondeur – figuraient en détail dans le plan directeur du quartier. Dans le cadre de ces contraintes, la conception a consisté à souligner un certain nombre de points liés à la ville. La courte façade donnant sur la place est traitée sous forme de deux tours, dont l'échelle monumentale caractérise cet espace public libre. » Recouvert de pierre naturelle, la pietra dorata, l'immeuble est un rectangle à indentations verticales aiguës sur trois côtés. Les façades les plus longues s'ornent de cinq rangées de hautes fenêtres verticales des deux côtés d'un retrait central.

Although the axonometric drawing above clearly shows that the volume of the structure is single, the treatment of the façade (detail to the right) gives the impression that there are two blocks.

Die Axonometrie zeigt zwar deutlich, daß es sich bei diesem Gebäude um einen einzigen frei stehenden Baukörper handelt, die Fassadengestaltung (rechts, Detail) läßt aus einem bestimmten Blickwinkel jedoch den Eindruck entstehen, es handele sich um zwei Bauteile.

Si la représentation axonométrique ci-dessus montre bien que la structure ne se compose que d'un seul volume, le traitement de la façade (détail à droite) donne l'impression de deux blocs.

Botta succeeds here again in creating a form that is exceptionally strong and yet not out of place in its setting. As the bank sits on a corner, it offers two distinct façades, one marked by numerous rectangular windows, the other by notches and two large square openings.

Botta ist es hier gelungen, eine Form zu schaffen, die zwar ungewöhnlich und dominant ist, aber dennoch nicht aus dem kontextuellen Rahmen fällt. Die Fassaden unterscheiden sich deutlich voneinander: Reihen identischer Fensteröffnungen gliedern die Längsseiten, hammerförmige Einschnitte und zwei ebenso breite Öffnungen auf Straßenniveau die Platzfront.

Botta réussit ici à créer une forme qui n'est pas déplacée par rapport à son contexte tout en affirmant une présence hors de l'ordinaire. Située à un angle de rue, la banque offre deux façades distinctes, l'une animée par de nombreuses fenêtres rectangulaires, l'autre par des découpes et deux grandes ouvertures carrées.

Interior detailing recalls the power of the axial
symmetry already introduced by the architect in
his façade designs. Contrasts between light and
dark form and articulate the space.

Die Innenarchitektur greift die kraftvolle
Axialsymmetrie auf, die auch für die Fassaden-
gestaltungen des Architekten so typisch ist.
Kontraste zwischen Hell und Dunkel formen
und gliedern den Raum.

À l'intérieur, se retrouve la même puissante
symétrie axiale imposée à la façade par l'architecte. Les contrastes entre l'ombre et la lumière
donnent forme à l'espace et à ses articulations.

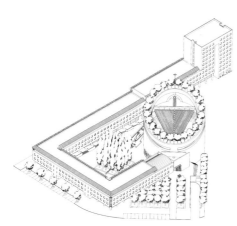

Cathedral
Evry, France, 1988–1995

Commissioned by the Diocese of Evry near Paris, this is the first cathedral built in France in over a century. It has an unusual circular design with an external diameter of 38.4 meters and an internal diameter of 29.3 meters. Because of the truncated roof, which admits ample natural light to the church, the overall height of the structure varies between 17 meters at its lowest point and 34 at its highest, with a ring of trees surrounding the skylight. A reinforced concrete building, it is clad inside and out with 800,000 bricks made in Toulouse. The interior benches, which seat 800 persons at ground level and 400–500 more in upper galleries, are made of Burgundy oak, and, like the white Carrara marble altar and baptismal font, were designed by the architect. Botta's cathedral, which functions as a signal of the city center, visible from the exit of the nearby A6 highway, together with an adjoining housing complex that he also designed, succeeds in giving Evry a certain "sense of place".

Die Kathedrale von Evry ist der einzige Sakralbau dieser Größe, der in den letzten 100 Jahren in Frankreich errichtet wurde. Den Auftrag dazu erteilte die Diözese von Evry. Die Kathedrale hat eine ungewöhnliche Form: Sie ist kreisrund (38,4 m Durchmesser außen und 29,3 m innen), und aufgrund der schrägen Dachfläche variiert ihre Höhe zwischen 17 m am tiefsten und 34 m am höchsten Punkt. Bäume umgeben das große Oberlicht im Dach. Die Konstruktion besteht aus Stahlbeton; ummantelt wurde der Sakralbau innen wie außen mit 800 000 Ziegelsteinen aus einer Toulouser Ziegelei. Die Kirchenbänke, auf denen im Kirchenschiff 800 und auf den oberen Galerien weitere 400 bis 500 Personen Platz finden, sind aus Burgunder Eiche gefertigt – ebenso nach Entwürfen des Architekten wie der Altar und das Taufbecken aus weißem Carrara-Marmor. Bottas Kathedrale, die das Stadtzentrum markiert, ist eine ebenfalls von ihm errichtete Wohnanlage angeschlossen. Beide Bauten verleihen der Stadt Evry ihren »Ortssinn«.

Commandée par le diocèse d'Evry, non loin de Paris, c'est la première cathédrale construite en France depuis un siècle. Elle présente un plan circulaire très inhabituel (diamètre extérieur : 38,4 m, diamètre intérieur : 29,3 m). Du fait de son toit tronqué qui laisse pénétrer une lumière généreuse dans la nef, sa hauteur varie entre 17 et 34 m. La verrière zénithale est entourée d'un cercle d'arbres. En béton armé, le bâtiment est recouvert à l'intérieur comme à l'extérieur de 800 000 briques fabriquées à Toulouse. Les bancs qui peuvent accueillir 800 fidèles au rez-de-chaussée et 4 à 500 supplémentaires dans les tribunes sont en chêne de Bourgogne. Comme l'autel de marbre blanc de Carrare et les fonts baptismaux, ils ont été dessinés par l'architecte. Cette cathédrale sert de signal au centre de la ville d'Evry. Elle est visible de la sortie de l'autoroute A6, de même que l'ensemble de logements que Botta a construit sur la même place, et donne à Evry un certain « sens du lieu ».

As the axonometric drawing to the left shows, the cathedral itself is part of a large diocesan complex. Like the church in Mogno, the cathedral has a truncated cylindrical form with an angled skylight. The long, low surrounding buildings serve to accentuate the height of the cathedral, topped by its unusual ring of trees (pp. 96/97).

Die axonometrische Darstellung zeigt, daß die Kathedrale zu einem großen Gebäudekomplex gehört. Auch diese Kirche hat die Form eines schräg abgeschnittenen Zylinders mit großem oculus. Die langgestreckten, niedrigen Nachbarbauten betonen noch die Höhe der Kathedrale mit ihrer ungewöhnlichen Baumkrone (S. 96/97).

Comme le montre la représentation axonométrique de gauche, la cathédrale fait partie d'un complexe diocésain. De la même manière que dans l'église de Mogno, la cathédrale est en forme de cylindre tronqué à toit-verrière incliné. Les longs bâtiments bas qui l'entourent accentuent l'effet de hauteur de la cathédrale, surmontée d'un curieux anneau d'arbres (pp. 96/97).

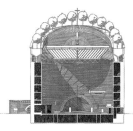
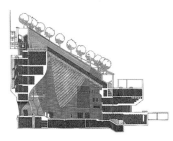
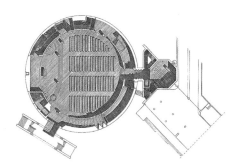

The very unusual interior of this cathedral is marked by furniture designed by Mario Botta, including the baptismal font, altar and pews. Above, two sections and a floor plan show the circular design executed in the form of a truncated cylinder.

Kirchengestühl, Taufbecken, Altar und Kanzel gehen auf Entwürfe Bottas zurück. Oben: zwei Querschnitte des Zylinderstumpfs mit Bäumen auf der Umfassungsmauer; Grundriß des Erdgeschosses.

Dans ce très inhabituel intérieur de cathédrale, le mobilier dessiné par Mario Botta – dont les fonts baptismaux, l'autel et les banquettes – ne laisse pas indifférent. Ci-dessus, deux coupes et le plan au sol illustrent le plan circulaire et sa projection en cylindre tronqué.

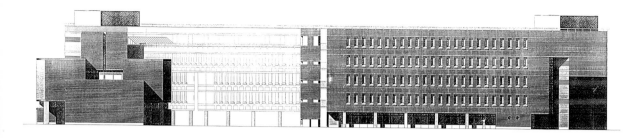

Swisscom Administration Center

Bellinzona, Ticino, Switzerland, 1988–1998

Insisting on the urban aspect of his work, Mario Botta says that this 27,800 square meter office complex located in the Colombaia area on the outskirts of Bellinzona should be considered as a "new point of reference for the evolution of this part of the city." A reinforced concrete structure with external cladding in red brick, the quadrilateral design with sides measuring 100 meters in length has a very large circular courtyard opening out in the direction of the historic castles of the city to the north. Mario Botta has chosen to emphasize the bulk of the building in opposition to the small scale of surrounding structures. Thus, the exterior façades are for the most part a full story higher than the circular band of offices facing the courtyard. As is often the case in his work, Mario Botta emphasizes the powerful axial design by placing a large rectangular opening on the inner façade of the circle directly in line with the entrance to the complex.

Immer wieder hebt Botta die städtebaulichen Aspekte seiner Architektur hervor und hat über dieses im Colombaia-Bezirk, am Rande von Bellinzona gelegene und 27 800 m² Gesamtfläche umfassende Bürogebäude der Swisscom AG geäußert, es solle als »neuer Bezugspunkt für die weitere Entwicklung dieses Stadtteils« dienen. Das Tragwerk besteht aus Stahlbeton, die Fassadenverkleidung aus roten Ziegelsteinen. Eingeschrieben in den 100 x 100 m messenden Block ist ein großer kreisrunder Innenhof, der sich zu den Burgen im Norden der Stadt hin öffnet. Anstatt den Eindruck von Massigkeit abzuschwächen, betont Botta bewußt dessen Kontrast mit der kleinteiligen Struktur seiner Umgebung. Die Außenfassaden des Verwaltungszentrums erheben sich zum größten Teil um ein ganzes Stockwerk über das Rund der Büros, die um den Innenhof angelegt sind. Der Architekt akzentuiert auch hier die kraftvolle axiale Ausrichtung dadurch, daß er in die Fassade, die zur Piazza gerichtet ist, eine große rechteckige Öffnung einfügte, die auf einer Achse mit dem Haupteingang liegt.

Mario Botta insiste sur l'aspect urbanistique de ses interventions. De cet ensemble de bureaux de 27 800 m² situé dans le quartier de Colombaia dans la banlieue de Bellinzona, il pense qu'il doit être considéré « comme un nouveau point de référence pour l'évolution de cette partie de la ville ». Structure en béton armé plaquée de brique rouge, ce quadrilatère de 100 m de long possède une très vaste cour intérieure circulaire s'ouvrant au nord vers les châteaux historiques de la ville. Plutôt que de tenter de minimiser sa masse, Botta a préféré la mettre en valeur par opposition aux petites constructions qui l'entourent. Ainsi, les façades extérieures sont pour leur plus grande part d'un étage plus haut que la façade intérieure circulaire. L'architecte a renforcé le puissant effet de symétrie en créant une importante ouverture rectangulaire sur la façade intérieure, dans l'axe de l'entrée du Centre administratif des Télécommunications.

Despite its large scale, this structure is made warmer by its brick cladding. Botta's early models and drawings showed trees on the roof of the area surrounding the central ring forming the courtyard, whereas the central bridge was absent.

Der große Verwaltungsbau vermittelt aufgrund seiner Ziegelsteinfassade den Eindruck von Wärme. Die ersten Modelle und Zeichnungen Bottas zeigen, daß er ursprünglich Bäume auf dem Dach vorgesehen hatte, während die Brücke im Innenhof noch fehlte.

Le parement de brique donne un peu de chaleur à ce bâtiment de très grandes dimensions. Les premières maquettes et dessins de Mario Botta faisaient apparaître des arbres sur le toit autour de l'anneau central qui constitue la cour. Le pont n'était pas encore prévu.

Although obviously at ease in its urban environment, which is dominated by modern architecture, the structure nonetheless stands out as a
singularly powerful gesture.

Der Neubau der Swisscom paßt sich zwar
gut in die Architektur seiner städtischen Umgebung ein, hebt sich aber aufgrund seiner ungewöhnlichen Gestalt und Ausdruckskraft auch
deutlich von ihr ab.

Bien qu'à l'aise dans son environnement
urbain dominé par des réalisations architecturales modernes, la structure de Botta ne s'en
distingue pas moins par son geste plein de force.

102 **Swisscom Administration Center**, Bellinzona

If the strict regularity of the fenestration brings to
mind some of the austere designs of the Italian
Rationalists, Botta's use of grass, trees and the
central bridge orders the composition in a more
humanist way.

Wenn die strenge Regelmäßigkeit der Fen-
sterung an die Entwürfe der italienischen Ratio-
nalisten denken läßt, so verleiht Bottas Gestaltung des Innenhofs mit Rasen, Bäumen und
zentraler Brücke dem Ensemble doch mehr
Menschlichkeit.

Si la stricte régularité du fenêtrage rappelle
certains austères projets de rationalistes italiens,
l'utilisation par Botta des pelouses, des arbres et
du pont central crée un ordonnancement plus
humain.

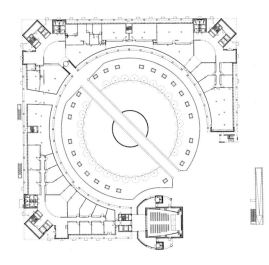

The central courtyard brings a measure of pro-
tected calm to the building, regardless of the nature of the immediate urban environment. Large
openings provide ample daylight to areas such as
the entrance lobby.

Der große zentrale Innenhof des Gebäude-
komplexes bietet Ruhe und Schutz vor dem
hektischen Treiben in seiner unmittelbaren Umgebung. Räume wie die Eingangshalle werden
über großflächige Verglasungen mit Tageslicht
durchflutet.

La cour centrale apporte un sentiment de
protection et de calme, sans se soucier de la nature de son environnement urbain immédiat.
De vastes ouvertures éclairent généreusement
certaines zones, comme l'atrium de l'entrée.

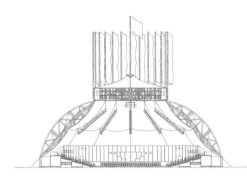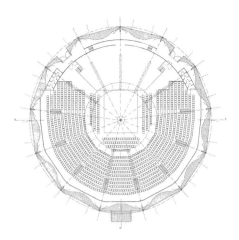

Tent for the Celebration of the 700th Anniversary of the Swiss Confederation
Switzerland, 1989–1991

"I imagined a structure capable of representing a primary image in the land-scape," says Mario Botta, "a cupola – something simple and precise, at once current and ancient and thus able to resist the confused jargon of fragile 'modern' culture." Commissioned by the Swiss Departments of the Interior and of Public Commerce, this project originated with a request for a large, unadorned tent to be placed in the central courtyard of the castle in Bellinzona, the capital of the Canton of Ticino, to celebrate the 700th anniversary of the Swiss Confederation. Seating 1,500 persons in an area of 1,540 square meters, the tent is supported by 13 painted white tubular steel ribs in the shape of half moons that break down into three components, facilitating transport and reassembly. The architect set the 26 flags of the cantons on top of the tent in a tight circle, giving an almost medieval air to this fundamentally modern structure.

»Mir schwebte eine Konstruktion vor«, so Botta, »die ein elementares Zeichen in die Landschaft setzen würde; eine Kuppel, etwas Einfaches und Präzises, zugleich zeitgenössisch und urtüm-lich und daher in der Lage, dem konfusen Jargon unserer zerbrechlichen ›modernen‹ Kultur etwas entgegen-zusetzen.« Botta entwickelte dieses Projekt – eine Auftragsarbeit der Schweizerischen Departemente für Inneres und Volkswirtschaft – als seine Antwort auf die Aufgabe, ein großes schmuckloses Zelt für die 700-Jahrfeiern der Eidgenossenschaft zu entwerfen, das im zentralen Burghof des Castelgrande von Bellinzona, der Hauptstadt des Kantons Tessin, errichtet werden könnte. Das Zelt verfügt über 1 500 Sitzplätze auf einer Fläche von 1 540 m². 13 mondsichelförmige, weißlackierte Stahlrohrrippen bilden sein Stützgerüst. Transport und Montage des Zelts werden insofern erleichtert, als die einzelnen Gerüstbögen drei Gelenke haben. Der Architekt setzte die 26 schweizerischen Kantonsflaggen ganz dicht beieinander in einem Kreis auf das Zelt, was dieser grundlegend modernen Konstruktion ein beinahe mittelalterliches Gepräge verlieh.

« J'ai imaginé une structure qui impose son image basique dans le paysage, quelque chose de simple et de précis, à la fois actuel et traditionnel, et donc capable de faire front devant le jargon confus de la culture dite moderne », commente Botta. Réalisé pour les ministères de l'Intérieur et du Commerce, ce projet était au départ une simple commande de tente pour la cour centrale du château de Bellinzona, capitale du canton du Tessin, à l'occasion des célébrations du 700ème anniversaire de la Con-fédération Helvétique. Comptant 1 500 places assises pour une surface de 1 540 m², elle est soutenue par 13 nervures d'acier tubulaire peintes en blanc en forme de demi-lune, composées de trois éléments afin de faciliter leur transport et leur assemblage. L'architecte a planté en cercle les 26 drapeaux des cantons ce qui donne un air presque médiéval à cette structure par ailleurs fondamentalement moderne.

The simple, circular form of the tent is by no means unexpect-ed, but the detailing, and in particular the numerous flags representing the Swiss cantons, give an unusual medieval air to a very modern structure in-tended to celebrate the 700th anniversary of the Swiss Con-federation.

Botta wählte die schlichte Kreisform für das Festzelt, in dem die Feierlichkeiten zum 700. Geburtstag der Schwei-zerischen Eidgenossenschaft stattfinden sollten; über-raschend ist die Flaggenkrone aus den Schweizer Kantons-fahnen auf dem Dach, die dem hochmodernen Bauwerk ein mittelalterliches Flair gibt.

La forme circulaire simple de la tente n'est certes pas inattendue, mais sa réalisation et en particulier les nombreux drapeaux des cantons suisses donnent un curieux air médié-val à cette très moderne struc-ture conçue pour les célébra-tions du 700ème anniversaire de la Confédération Helvétique.

Botta's own sketches (left, above) show the rapport between the tent and the ancient castle
architecture. The tent is equally at home by the
lakeside, however as demonstrated in the picture
above.

Bottas Skizzen zeigen den Bezug zwischen
Zelt und alter Burgarchitektur (oben links). Das
Zelt könnte jedoch genausogut an einem See
aufgebaut werden (oben).

Les croquis de Botta illustrent le rapport
entre la tente et le château médiéval (en haut à
gauche). La tente s'adapte tout aussi bien à un
site en bordure d'un lac, comme le montre la
photo ci-dessus.

Single Family House
Daro-Bellinzona, Ticino, Switzerland, 1989–1992

The house has a rather unusual plan, which is related to its location on a steep hillside overlooking the area of Bellinzona. Its shape resembles that of an iron or a wedge, with its point facing the hill. The façade facing outward is flat with a curved spaceframe arcing over the heart of the 230 square meter house. The reinforced concrete walls are clad in gray cement blocks, with some placed at a 45° angle to give the main façade a distinct relief. The main doorway is defined by a tall, high incision into the main façade, and is located directly on the main axis of the plan. The rather closed and defensive posture of the architecture at entrance level becomes progressively lighter and more open, culminating in the spaceframe above. Black slate is used for the interior floors and granite slabs outside. The house measures 12.6 meters in depth by 9.9 meters in width, and is 7.5 meters high.

Das Einfamilienhaus von Daro weist einen relativ ungewöhnlichen Grundriß auf, der sich aus seiner Lage auf einem stark abschüssigen Grundstück ergibt. Von seiner Form her erinnert es an ein Bügeleisen oder einen Keil, dessen Spitze zum Hang gerichtet ist. Die von diesem abgewandte Fassade ist eben; ein bogenförmiges Raumfachwerk überfängt die Mitte des 230 m² Wohnfläche umfassenden Gebäudes. Die Stahlbetonwände sind mit zum Teil im Winkel von 45° eingesetzten grauen Zementsteinen verkleidet, die der Hauptfassade ihre besondere Struktur verleihen. Den Eingang markiert ein hoher, schmaler Wandeinschnitt, der sich exakt auf der Hauptachse des Grundrisses befindet. Das im vorderen Bereich eher defensiv, verschlossen, fast hermetisch wirkende Haus wird zum Hügel hin zunehmend leichter und offener; ihren Höhepunkt erreicht diese Gestaltung mit dem Raumfachwerkbogen. Schwarzer Schiefer bedeckt die Böden der Innenräume. Terrassen und Wege sind mit Granitplatten belegt. Das Haus mit Blick über das Stadtgebiet von Bellinzona mißt 7,5 m in der Höhe, 9,9 m in der Breite und 12,6 m in der Tiefe.

La maison familiale de 230 m² doit un plan assez inhabituel à son implantation au flanc d'une colline escarpée dans les hauteurs de Bellinzona. Sa forme fait penser à un fer à repasser ou un coin, dont la pointe ferait face à la colline. La façade est plate vers l'extérieur tandis qu'une structure incurvée recouvre le centre de la maison. Les murs en béton armé sont plaqués de parpaings de ciment gris dont certains sont orientés à 45° pour créer un motif en relief. En façade, l'embrasure de la porte est définie par une incision dans l'axe principal. L'aspect assez fermé et défensif que l'on ressent à l'entrée s'allège et s'ouvre peu à peu, pour culminer dans la structure tridimensionnelle du toit. Les sols sont en ardoise noire à l'intérieur et en dalle de granit à l'extérieur. La maison familiale mesure 12,6 m de profondeur, 9,9 de large et 7,5 de haut.

As he did in his Single Family House, Morbio Superiore, Botta enriches the façade of this house by patterning the façade, laying some blocks at a 45° angle. The metallic arch over the house also brings to mind his commercial building at Lugano-Paradiso, albeit on a smaller scale.

Wie bei dem Einfamilienhaus in Morbio Superiore schmückte Botta auch bei diesem Haus die Fassade mit einem Mauerrelief aus Bändern von schräg und bündig gemauerten Ziegelsteinen. Der Raumfachwerkbogen erinnert an das Büro- und Geschäftshaus in Lugano-Paradiso.

Comme dans sa résidence familiale de Morbio Superiore, Botta anime la façade de cette maison d'un motif géométrique en disposant des rangées de parpaings à 45° les uns par rapport aux autres. La structure métallique du toit rappelle l'immeuble de Lugano-Paradiso, bien qu'à plus petite échelle.

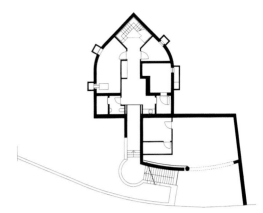

The wedge-like plan (right) is not visible from the front of the house, but serves to anchor it firmly in the steep hillside. As is usually the case with Botta, the determined axiality of the façade is echoed strongly in the interior.

Von der Straße aus ist nicht zu erkennen, daß dieses Haus im Plan (rechts) wie ein abgerundeter Keil ist, dessen Spitze das Gebäude fest im Hang verankert. Wie meistens bei Bauten von Botta, setzt sich die Axialsymmetrie der Fassade im Innern fort.

La forme en coin du plan (à droite) n'est pas perceptible de la façade principale de la maison, mais sert à ancrer celle-ci dans la pente raide de la colline. Comme d'habitude chez Botta, l'axialité appuyée de la façade trouve un écho dans l'aménagement de l'intérieur.

Museum of Modern Art

San Francisco, California, USA, 1989–1995

"In a contemporary city," says Mario Botta, "the museum is elevated to the status of a new cathedral, a place for the memory of and relationship with other epochs, as filtered through the works of art exhibited. But it is also an urban focus." Entirely clad in brick, his Museum of Modern Art in the Yerba Buena district of San Francisco has a net floor area of 20,900 square meters. The most characteristic feature of the building is the truncated cylinder that emerges from the top and rises to a height of 44 meters above street level. A skylight brings natural light into the upper galleries, but also down to the entrance level. The first gallery floor, with its 5-meter ceilings, houses selections from the permanent collection, and provides space for the architecture and design departments. A more intimate second gallery floor displays photographs and works on paper. The top two floors, with very high 5.5- and 7.2-meter ceilings, are designed for special temporary exhibitions and large-scale contemporary art from the museum's permanent collection.

»In der zeitgenössischen Stadt«, so Mario Botta, »erhält das Museum den Status einer neuen Kathedrale; es wird zu einem Ort der Erinnerung an andere Epochen erhoben, an dem man einen Bezug zur Geschichte findet, wie sie sich durch den Filter der hier gezeigten Kunstwerke darstellt. Es ist aber auch ein städtischer Brennpunkt.« Das Museum, vollständig mit Ziegelsteinen verkleidet, hat eine Gesamtfläche von 20 900 m². Besonders auffällig ist der zentrale, abgeschrägte Zylinder, der sich bis zu einer Höhe von 44 m erhebt. Ein rundes Dachoberlicht läßt Licht bis in die Eingangsebene fallen. Die Räume im ersten Geschoß sind 5 m hoch und beherbergen Teile der ständigen Sammlung sowie die Abteilungen Architektur und Design. Eine weitere Ebene mit kleineren Räumen zeigt Fotografien und Arbeiten auf Papier. Die beiden oberen Geschosse mit Raumhöhen von 5,5 und 7,2 m sind für Sonderausstellungen und großformatige zeitgenössische Kunstwerke der ständigen Sammlung vorgesehen.

« Dans une ville contemporaine », explique Mario Botta, « le musée est élevé au statut de cathédrale, de lieu de mémoire et de relations avec les autres époques, représentées par les œuvres d'art exposées. Mais c'est aussi un centre d'attraction pour la ville. » Entièrement plaqué de brique, ce musée édifié dans le quartier de Yerba Buena à San Francisco est un vaste bâtiment de 20 900 m². Sa caractéristique la plus frappante est le cylindre tronqué qui émerge du toit et s'élève à 44 m de haut. Sa verrière dispense la lumière naturelle des galeries supérieures au hall d'entrée. Le premier niveau de galeries, de 5 m de haut, abrite une sélection des collections permanentes ainsi que les départements d'architecture et de design. Le second étage, plus intime, est réservé à la photographie et aux œuvres sur papier. Les deux derniers niveaux, dont les plafonds élevés atteignent 5,5 et 7,2 m, sont destinés aux expositions temporaires et aux grandes pièces d'art contemporain de la collection permanente.

Botta's sketch makes clear the proportion of the museum to neighboring towers, but does not really take into account the buildings by Fumihiko Maki and James Stewart Polshek located in the foreground of the photo on the right. This side view (pp. 116/117) shows the entrance to the museum, with the tall buildings of downtown San Francisco in the background. This angle also makes the rather massive aspect of the museum seem appropriate.

Bottas Skizze verdeutlicht die Größenverhältnisse des Museums in bezug auf die Bauten seiner Umgebung. Allerdings führt er die Bauten von Fumihiko Maki und James Stewart Polshek (Foto rechts, im Vordergrund) darin nicht auf. Aus diesem Blickwinkel (S. 116/117), vor dem Hintergrund der Hochhäuser von Downtown San Francisco, erscheint die Massivität des Gebäudes durchaus angebracht.

Le croquis de Botta (ci-dessus) précise les proportions du musée par rapport aux tours avoisinantes, mais ne prend pas vraiment en compte les bâtiments de Fumihiko Maki et de James Stewart Polshek, au premier plan de la photo de droite. La vue latérale (pp. 116/117) montre l'entrée sur Third Street, sur fond de tours de bureaux, angle de vision qui justifie également l'aspect assez massif de ce musée.

On the left, the lobby area of the museum draws light from the central oculus far above. Wherever conservation of the works of art permits, and particularly in the upper galleries, Botta has called on natural overhead lighting.

Links die Eingangshalle des Museums, die durch das Opäum Tageslicht von oben erhält. Im gesamten Museum, und besonders in den Galerien des obersten Geschosses, hat Botta Tageslichtbeleuchtung durch Oberlichter vorgesehen, soweit es konservatorische Vorgaben erlaubten.

À gauche, l'atrium d'entrée du musée tire son éclairage de l'oculus central, situé plusieurs niveaux plus haut. Dans la mesure où les œuvres le permettent, et en particulier dans les galeries supérieures, Botta a privilégié l'éclairage zénithal naturel.

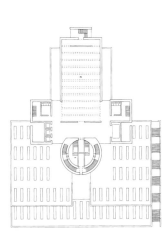

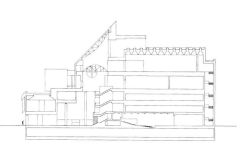

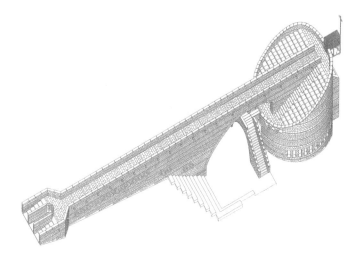

Chapel

Monte Tamaro, Ticino, Switzerland, 1990–1996

Designed and built when Mario Botta was involved in his controversial plans for the church in Mogno, the Santa Maria degli Angeli Chapel is located at an altitude of 2,000 meters above the highway that links Bellinzona to Lugano. Egidio Cattaneo, the owner of the lifts leading up to the ski resort at the Monte Tamaro, was taken by Botta's scheme for Mogno, and asked him to build a chapel in memory of his wife. Its rugged power is defined not only by its strong forms, but also by its unusual cladding of rusticated porphyry. The whole is completed by a group of frescoes by the Italian painter Enzo Cucchi, who was in tune with the spiritual nature of the architect's scheme. He has painted a large pair of hands behind the altar. Lit from above by natural light they appear to be ready to gather up the faithful. Both the chapel itself and its decor are indisputably modern, and yet they also appear to have roots in ancient or Romanesque architecture.

Die Kapelle Santa Maria degli Angeli auf dem Monte Tamaro plante und realisierte Botta parallel zu seiner Arbeit am umstrittenen Entwurf für die Dorfkirche von Mogno. Das Bauwerk steht auf einer Höhe von 2 000 Metern ü.d.M. oberhalb der Autobahn, die Bellinzona mit Lugano verbindet. Egidio Cattaneo war fasziniert von Bottas Konzept für Mogno und beauftragte ihn mit dem Entwurf und dem Bau einer Kapelle zum Gedenken an seine verstorbene Frau. Die rauhe, kraftvolle Schlichtheit, die den Sakralbau auszeichnet, beruht nicht nur auf seinen massiven Formen, sondern auch auf den grob behauenen Porphyr-steinen der Fassaden. Der italienische Maler Enzo Cucchi hat die Spiritualität von Bottas architektonischem Entwurf kongenial erfaßt. In seinem Fresko, hinter dem Altar, stellt er zwei große Hände dar. Das von oben einfallende Licht erweckt den Eindruck, als seien sie aufnahmebereit – bereit, die Gläubigen aufzunehmen. Sowohl die Konstruktion als auch die künstlerische Ausstattung sind unbestreitbar modern und scheinen doch gleichzeitig tief in der romanischen Architektur verwurzelt zu sein.

Dessinée et construite pendant la controverse sur l'église de Mogno, la chapelle Sainte-Marie-des-Anges est située à 2 000 m au-dessus de l'autoroute qui relie Bellinzona et Lugano. Egidio Cattaneo, propriétaire des remontées mécaniques qui desservent les pistes de ski du Monte Tamaro avait été séduit par le projet de Botta pour Mogno et lui avait demandé d'édifier une chapelle en mémoire de son épouse. Sa puissance brute naît non seulement de ses formes massives, mais aussi de son parement original de porphyre rustiqué. L'ensemble est complété par un groupe de fresques du peintre italien Enzo Cucchi, en accord avec la nature spirituelle de la création architecturale. L'artiste a représenté d'énormes mains derrière l'autel. Éclairées par la lumière naturelle, ces fresques semblent accueillir les fidèles. La chapelle et son décor sont indiscutablement modernes mais semblent néanmoins prendre leurs racines dans l'architecture antique et romane.

An axonometric drawing shows the unusual long form of the chapel, with its narrow approach ramp. The rusticated porphyry cladding accentuates the impression that this architectural form is at once quite modern and very ancient. In its spectacular mountain setting, this chapel offers views of the mountains (pp. 122/123) at the same time as it seems to draw its force from the very stone that surrounds it.

Die axonometrische Dar-stellung zeigt die ungewöhnlich langgestreckte Form der Kapelle samt ihrer schmalen Zugangsrampe. Das Mauerwerk besteht aus grob behauenen Porphyrsteinen. Von der Kirche aus – die ihre Kraft aus den Steinen der Umgebung zu beziehen scheint – ist eine Panoramasicht auf die Bergwelt zu genießen (S. 122/123).

La représentation axonométrique montre la forme étonnamment longue de la chapelle et son étroite rampe d'approche. Le parement en porphyre rustiqué accentue l'impression simultanée de modernité et d'ancienneté de cette forme architecturale. La chapelle offre des vues spectaculaires sur les montagnes et semble tirer sa force du rocher qui l'entoure (pp. 122/123).

The visitor who takes the long roof ramp to the
small observation point near the black metal
cross has the feeling of being suspended above
the mountain valley.

Wer die lange Rampe zum Aussichtspunkt
mit dem schwarzen Metallkreuz hinaufgeht, hat
das Gefühl, zwischen Berg und Tal in der Luft zu
schweben.

Le visiteur qui emprunte la longue rampe
d'accès au belvédère (près de la croix de métal
noir) a le sentiment de se trouver en suspension
au-dessus de la vallée.

Botta's sketch shows the peak of Monte Tamaro in the background, and passes over the lift facilities that are in fact quite clear to the left and right of the rear of the chapel. Below, the altar and works by Enzo Cucchi.

Die Skizze von Botta zeigt im Hintergrund den Gipfel des Monte Tamaro, davor in Serpentinen angedeutet das Skigebiet mit Liftgebäuden links und rechts hinter der Kapelle. Unten: Blick auf Altar und Fresko von Enzo Cucchi.

Le dessin de Botta montre le sommet du Monte Tamaro au fond, le passage de la remontée mécanique – en fait assez présente – à gauche, et à droite la face arrière de la chapelle. Ci-dessous, l'autel et les fresques d'Enzo Cucchi.

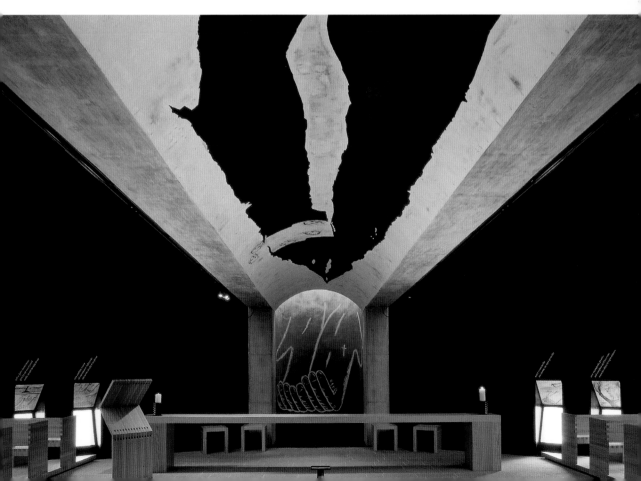

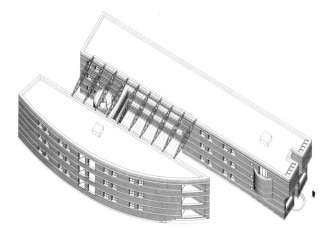

Housing

Monte Carasso, Ticino, Switzerland, 1992–1996

Located in a small town near Bellinzona that is characterized by the architecture of Luigi Snozzi, this housing complex offers 2,490 square meters of space for 30 apartments, and is clad in light gray exposed concrete blocks. One unusual feature is the large, white-painted, grid metal structure with a transparent polycarbonate strip roof that arches above the entrance space. The focal point of this area is a cylindrical volume that houses a stairwell. The central placement of this blank volume is unexpected, but does provide a focus for the arriving visitors, and accentuates a certain monumentality. The plan consists of one rectangular volume with circular protrusions, whose purpose is to house living room space, and another shape with a sweeping curved façade – the two brought together under the entrance canopy. A bright lighting system for the exterior of the building also accentuates its symbolic role in this town.

Der Komplex mit 30 Wohnungen (Gesamtfläche 2 490 m²) – in einer Kleinstadt bei Bellinzona, die geprägt ist von der Architektur Luigi Snozzis – ist mit hellgrauen Betonwerksteinen verkleidet. Ein ungewöhnliches Gestaltungselement ist die große weißlackierte Gitterkonstruktion mit transparenter Abdeckung aus Polycarbonatstreifen, die den Eingangsbereich überspannt. Im Zentrum dieser Zone erhebt sich der zylinderförmige Treppenhausturm. Die Plazierung eines solchen geschlossenen Volumens ist überraschend, bietet ankommenden Besuchern aber einen Orientierungspunkt und akzentuiert die Monumentalität des Gebäudes. Im Grundriß zeigt es ein Rechteck mit halbkreisförmigen Ausbuchtungen, die als Wohnräume dienen, und ein zweites Volumen mit einer sanft geschwungenen Fassade. Beide Baukörper werden unter dem Eingangsvordach zusammengeführt. Die Außenfassade des Gebäudes wird mittels eines speziellen Beleuchtungssystems illuminiert, was seine symbolische Funktion als herausragendes, leuchtendes Beispiel in dieser Stadt unterstreicht.

Situé dans une petite ville près de Bellinzona, marquée par l'architecture de l'architecte Luigi Snozzi, cet ensemble de logements de 2 490 m² compte 30 appartements. Il est recouvert de blocs de béton brut gris clair. Au-dessus de l'entrée se trouve une structure en arche métallique blanche à bandeau de polycarbonate transparent au-dessus de l'espace d'entrée. Cette zone est marquée par un volume cylindrique qui fait office de cage d'escalier. L'implantation centrale de ce volume aveugle est inattendue, mais crée un centre d'attraction pour les visiteurs et accentue une certaine monumentalité d'ensemble. Le plan consiste en un volume rectangulaire à avancées circulaires qui abritent les salles de séjour et un second volume en courbe qui se rejoignent sous l'auvent de l'entrée. Un système d'éclairage très visible à l'extérieur accentue le rôle symbolique que l'immeuble remplit pour la ville.

Although it still has an axial entrance canopy, this structure is fundamentally asymmetrical – an unusual situation in Botta's architecture – as can be seen in the axonometric drawing above. To the right, the rather massive central stairwell cylinder.

Der Bau hat zwar eine Mittelachse mit gewölbtem Glasdach über dem Eingang, ist aber ansonsten vollkommen asymmetrisch (s. Axonometrie) und damit eher ungewöhnlich für Bottas Architektur. Rechts der Treppenturm im Eingangsbereich.

Bien que dotée d'un auvent d'entrée axial, la structure du bâtiment est fondamentalement asymétrique, parti assez rare chez Botta, comme le montre la représentation axonométrique de gauche. À droite, le massif cylindre de la cage d'escalier centrale.

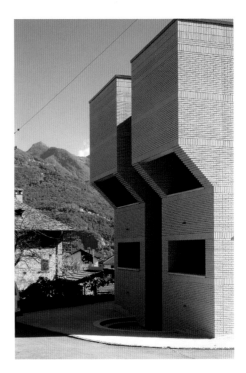

A wide-angle view emphasizes the elongated
curvature of the volume on the left, while mini-
mizing the mass of the whole.
*Die Weitwinkelaufnahme betont die Länge
des gekrümmten Gebäudeteils links, während sie
die Gesamtbaumasse optisch minimiert.*
*La vue au grand angle met en valeur la cour-
be tendue du volume de gauche, et minimise la
masse de l'ensemble.*

The building's powerful, solid presence stands out from its immediate environment with some echoes of surrounding volumes.

Das eindrucksvolle Gebäude hebt sich einerseits von seiner Umgebung ab, weist andererseits aber auch gewisse Ähnlichkeiten mit Nachbarbauten auf.

Sa puissance et sa massive présence détachent le bâtiment de son environnement immédiat non sans rappeler quelques volumes avoisinants.

Home for the Elderly
Novazzano, Ticino, Switzerland, 1992–1998

Erected near Botta's home town of Mendrisio, this rest home is designed around the idea of a circular structure, 49.24 meters in diameter, with 25 rooms per level on two floors. Net floor area is 3,271 square meters. Balcony windows look out onto the surrounding countryside, while the internal hallways are placed on the inner part of the circle. The circular form is notched at the entrance to provide space for a large portico, whose structure recalls a double-sized version of the ones Botta designed for Monte Carasso or the Housing and shop complex in Lugano. As Mario Botta says, "Residents are encouraged to converge along a corridor from their rooms towards communal areas in the center of the building. A double-height community space provides a space of interest and focus for the guests."

Der Standort des Seniorenwohnheims befindet sich nicht weit von Bottas Heimat- ort Mendrisio entfernt. Konzipiert ist der Bau als Ringform (49,24 m Durchmesser), die auf zwei Stockwerken je 25 Räume enthält. Die Gesamtfläche beträgt 3 271 m². Balkonfenster gewähren Ausblicke in die Landschaft, während die Korridore auf der Innenseite des Rings angelegt sind. Ein Einschnitt im Rund markiert den Ein- gangsbereich, dessen großer Portikus wie eine zweifache Vergrößerung derjenigen wirkt, die Botta für die Wohnanlage in Monte Carasso und das Wohn- und Geschäftshaus in Lugano entworfen hat. Botta selbst verbindet mit dem Gebäude folgende Vorstellung: »Die Heimbewohner werden dazu ermutigt, ihre Zimmer zu verlassen, um im Korridor zusammenzukommen und sich in die Gemeinschaftsräume in der Mitte des Hauses zu begeben. Ein über zwei Geschosse reichender großer Raum ist Anziehungspunkt für Bewohner und Besucher.«

Située non loin de la ville natale de Botta, Mendrisio, cette maison de retraite est conçue sur le principe d'une structure circulaire de 49,24 m de diamètre. Elle compte 25 chambres sur deux niveaux, pour une surface totale de 3 271 m². Les fenêtres des balcons donnent sur la campagne environnante, et les halls intérieurs sont disposés dans la partie intérieure du cercle. La forme circulaire est découpée à l'entrée pour laisser place à un vaste portique, dont la structure rappelle en deux fois plus grand, celles dessi- nées par Botta pour Monte Carasso ou l'ensemble de logements et de commerces de Lugano. Comme le pré- cise l'architecte : « Les résidents sont incités à utiliser un corridor qui, à partir de leur chambre, les conduit aux parties communes au centre du bâtiment. Un espace communautaire à double hauteur offre un espace intéres- sant, qui attire l'attention des visiteurs. »

Here Botta returns to his fa- vored symmetrical profile, in a cylindrical form. Images such as the one above give an im- pression of rather empty surroundings.

Hier kehrt der Architekt zu der von ihm bevorzugten Axial- symmetrie zurück, allerdings in eine Zylinderform eingeschrie- ben (rechts oben). Die Aus- sichten auf den Fotos erwecken den Eindruck, als stehe das Seniorenheim relativ einsam in der Landschaft.

Retour à la symétrie à la- quelle l'architecte est attaché.

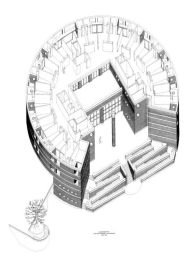

In the image below, the singular power so typical of Botta's smaller private houses is heightened by the strict symmetry and defining central column. Combining the regularity of his coffered ceiling and the ample height of this space (pp. 132/133), Botta hangs an array of lighting fixtures whose globular, clear form contrasts markedly with the solidity of the architecture.

In dieser Ansicht (unten) vermittelt der Bau die für Bottas Einfamilienhäuser so typische Ausdruckskraft einer strengen Symmetrie zu beiden Seiten der buchstäblich maßgebenden Mittelsäule. Den hohen Gemeinschaftsraum mit seiner Betonkassettendecke (S. 132/133) stattete Botta mit zahlreichen Hängeleuchten aus, deren Kugeln aus Klarglas einen deutlichen Kontrast zu der massiven, kantigen Baukonstruktion bilden.

Dans l'image ci-dessous, se retrouve la singulière impression de force qui émane des résidences privées dessinées par Botta, renforcée par une symétrie stricte et l'axe de la colonne centrale. Jouant de la régularité de la trame du plafond à caissons et de la grande hauteur du volume, il a imaginé un système d'éclairage (pp. 132/133) dont les globes et la transparence contrastent avec la massivité de l'architecture.

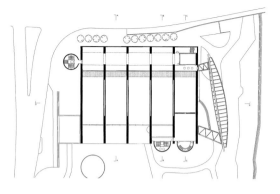

Museum Jean Tinguely
Basel, Switzerland, 1993–1996

With 2,866 square meters of exhibition space and a total area of 6,057 square meters, the new Museum Jean Tinguely was built thanks to the generosity of the pharmaceuticals giant F. Hoffmann-La Roche AG, and the widow of the artist Niki de Saint Phalle. It was erected on the premises of the corporation, on the banks of the Rhine, opposite the old city of Basel. The site, in many respects quite attractive, posed numerous architectural problems, such as the highway and rail link that passes directly next to the building. Built for a budget of 30 million Swiss francs, the structure is clad in pink Alsatian sandstone (Rosé de Champenay), which immediately differentiates it from Botta's brick buildings. In contrast to the ephemeral, scrap metal creations of Jean Tinguely, the architect chose the gray-tinted oak floors or Venetian black stucco used inside. The most spectacular architectural gesture seen in the museum is what Botta calls "La Barca" (the boat), a long, sloping glass gallery leading visitors into the museum as it offers them a view over the Rhine.

Mit seinen 2 866 m² Ausstellungsfläche und einer Gesamtfläche von 6 057 m² konnte das neue Museum Jean Tinguely dank der großzügigen Förderung durch den Pharmariesen F. Hoffmann-La Roche AG und die Witwe des Künstlers, Niki de Saint Phalle, realisiert werden. Es steht am Ufer des Rheins, gegenüber der Basler Altstadt, auf dem Gelände des Pharmaunternehmens. Obwohl der dort gelegene Park sehr attraktiv ist, bot er im Hinblick auf die Gestaltung des Gebäudes doch eine ganze Reihe von Schwierigkeiten, nicht zuletzt durch die unmittelbar daran vorbeiführende Autobahn und die Eisenbahnstrecke. Der Bau des mit rosafarbenem Elsässer Sandstein (Rosé de Champenay) verkleideten Museums kostete 30 Millionen Schweizer Franken. Für die Innenräume wählte der Architekt zum Teil hellgrau getönte Eichenstabparkettböden und venezianischen Stuck. Das auffälligste Gestaltungselement dieses Museums nennt Botta »La Barca« (das Schiff) – eine lange verglaste Außenrampe, parallel zum Rhein, über die die Besucher in das Museum gelangen.

Ce musée de 2 866 m² d'espaces d'exposition et de 6 057 m² de surface totale a été construit grâce à la générosité du groupe pharmaceutique Hoffmann-La Roche et de la veuve de l'artiste, Niki de Saint Phalle. Il a été érigé sur un terrain de l'entreprise, au bord du Rhin, face à l'ancien centre de Bâle. Bien que séduisant à de nombreux égards, le site posait de multiples problèmes architecturaux, dont la, présence d'une autoroute et de voies de chemin de fer à proximité immédiate. Construite pour un budget de 30 millions de francs suisses, la structure est plaquée de grès rose d'Alsace (Rosé de Champenay). Pour l'intérieur, en contraste volontaire avec les sculptures d'apparence éphémère et en matériaux métalliques de récupération de Jean Tinguely, l'architecte a choisi des sols en chêne teinté gris et un stuc vénitien noir pour les murs. Le geste architectural le plus spectaculaire est ce que Botta a appelé « La barca » (la barque), une longue coursive vitrée en pente qui mène les visiteurs au musée et leur offre une vue sur le fleuve.

A plan of the second floor, above, shows the curved shape of the "Barca" along the banks of the Rhine. This entrance ramp is visible in the photo to the right. Within the "Barca" itself (pp. 136/137), visitors approach the exhibition galleries. The architect has insisted that this space must remain entirely empty so as to retain the emphasis on the view.

Im Grundriß des zweiten Geschosses (oben) ist die Form der »Barke« am Rheinufer gut zu erkennen. Rechts die verglaste Zugangsrampe. Von ihrem Innern aus genießen die Besucher auf ihrem Weg zum Museumseingang den Blick auf den Fluß (S. 136/137). Der Architekt hat darauf bestanden, diesen Raum völlig leer zu belassen, damit nichts die Aussicht versperre.

Le plan du deuxième étage (ci-dessus), montre la forme incurvée de la « Barca » le long de la rive du Rhin. Cette rampe d'entrée est visible sur la photo de droite. Par la « Barca » qui donne sur le Rhin, le visiteur accède aux galeries d'exposition (pp. 136/137). L'architecte a voulu que cet espace reste entièrement vide pour laisser à la vue toute sa présence.

Above, on the park side, the museum is open to its very green environment. To the right (p. 139), the street-side façade, and below, the Rhine-side aspect of the museum with the "Barca" visible.

Auf der Parkseite (oben) öffnet sich das Museum und bietet einen Ausblick auf die Grünanlagen. Rechts (S.139) eine Ansicht der Straßenfassade (oben) und die Ansicht vom gegenüberliegenden Rheinufer her (unten) auf die »Barke«.

Ci-dessus, côté parc, le musée s'ouvre sur un environnement très vert. À droite (p.139), la façade côté rue, et ci-dessous la façade côté Rhin et la « Barca ».

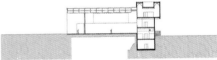

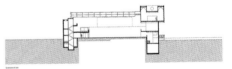

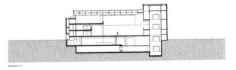

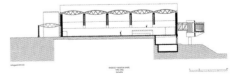

Part of the architect's mission in this instance was to create a vaste, open space for Jean Tinguely's large works. Mario Botta chose intentionally to limit both his palette and the architectural effects of the interior spaces so as to emphasize the works.

Ein Hauptanliegen des Architekten war es, einen großen Raum für Jean Tinguelys Großplastiken zu schaffen. Botta gestaltete ihn bewußt zurückhaltend, um den Skulpturen Vorrang vor der Architektur einzuräumen.

Une partie de la mission de l'architecte était de créer un vaste espace ouvert pour présenter les grandes œuvres de Tinguely. Mario Botta a volontairement choisi de limiter sa palette et les effets architecturaux des espaces intérieurs au profit des œuvres.

Looking out toward the park side of the museum where the "machines" of Tinguely are placed against a natural background, behind the high bank of windows whose form shows Botta's talent.

Blick durch einen Galerieraum in den Park. Tinguelys »Maschinen« sind auf einer Plattform vor »natürlicher Kulisse« aufgebaut. Hervorzuheben ist außerdem die ungewöhnliche Gliederung der Verglasungsrahmen.

Vue vers le parc dans lequel des « machines » de Tinguely sont disposées sur un fond naturel, de l'autre côté des grandes baies dont la forme illustre le talent de l'architecte.

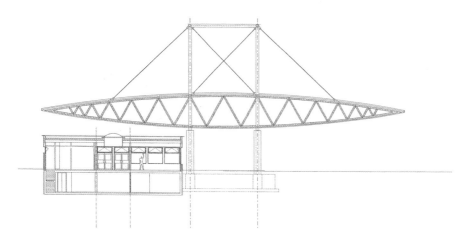

Service Station
Quinto, Ticino, Switzerland, 1993–1998

Winner of a 1993 design competition for this gas station, located near the southern mouth of the San Gotthard Tunnel, Mario Botta also worked on another unbuilt station design for Agip in France near Lyon the same year. In Quinto, the basic "airplane" wing design of the protective canopy above the actual gas pump areas and the station building is colored a bright enameled red, making the structure stand out against both the highway and the mountainous natural environment. The canopy measures 50 x 70 meters, and stands 10.5 meters above the ground. Set on a 46,500 square meter site, the station itself covers 1,130 square meters, and was built not for an oil company, but for the city of Quinto.

Zu dem Zeitpunkt, als Bottas Entwurf für diese Tankstelle am Südausgang des Sankt-Gotthard-Tunnels 1993 als Sieger aus dem dafür ausgelobten Wettbewerb hervorging, arbeitete der Architekt gerade an einem weiteren – allerdings nie realisierten – Tankstellenprojekt für Agip, und zwar für einen Standort in der Nähe von Lyon. In Quinto erhebt sich eine Art Flugzeugtragfläche, grellrot lackiert, mit aufgesetztem Stangengerüst, als Schutzdach über Zapfsäulen und Tankstellengebäude und setzt damit einen markanten Kontrastpunkt vor die Kulisse aus Autobahn und Alpenlandschaft. Das Dach mißt 50 x 70 m und befindet sich 10,5 m über dem Erdboden. Die Tankstelle überbaut 1 130 von insgesamt 46 500 m² Fläche und wurde vorrangig für die Ortschaft Quinto gebaut.

Après avoir remporté en 1993 le concours pour cette station d'essence située près de la sortie sud du tunnel du Saint-Gottard, Mario Botta a également travaillé la même année sur un second projet de station-service pour Agip en France, près de Lyon. À Quinto, le concept en aile d'avion de l'auvent qui protège les pompes et le bâtiment sont peints d'un émail rouge vif qui les fait ressortir sur le paysage de l'autoroute et son environnement montagneux naturel. Cet auvent mesure 50 x 70 m pour une hauteur de 10,5 m. Sur un terrain de 46 500 m², la station occupe 1 130 m² et a été construite non pour une compagnie pétrolière, mais pour la commune de Quinto.

The lightweight frame structure of the station serves naturally to protect customers and their vehicles, but it also constitutes the "signature" element that makes it clear that this is no ordinary roadside stop.

Die Leichtrahmenkonstruktion des Tankstellengebäudes ist einerseits Schutzdach, bildet andererseits aber auch das »Erkennungsmerkmal« dieser ungewöhnlichen Tank- und Raststätte.

La structure légère de la station-service protège les clients et leurs véhicules, mais confère également une personnalité certaine à cet équipement routier.

In its majestic mountain setting the station nonetheless stands out, thanks to its prominent highway location. The powerful simplicity and bright color of the station make it all the more visible.

Die Autobahntankstelle im Tal fällt nicht nur ihrer Form wegen, sondern auch aufgrund ihrer kräftigen Farben auf.

Dans son majestueux cadre de montagnes, la station-service met à profit sa situation en bordure de l'autoroute. Elle assure sa visibilité par sa simplicité, sa force et ses couleurs éclatantes.

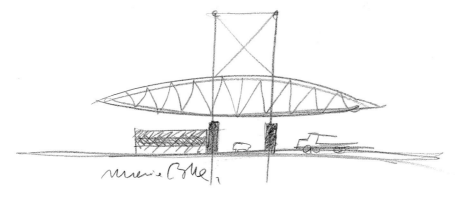

Municipal Library
Dortmund, Germany, 1995–1998

Characterized by a stepped rectangular main volume with a large semicircular form emerging from its façade, this library has a gross floor area of 14,130 square meters. The entrance is located in the truncated cone, whose lower radius is 25.9 meters, increasing to 29.5 meters at the top. As Mario Botta says, "The design aims to consolidate the urban front of the city at the exit to the railway station. That is why the new building is divided into two distinct parts: a massive austere red stone linear volume re-establishing the walled front and a truncated glass cone, protruding from the alignment, to be used as the reading room and leisure facility." The architect readily agrees that large glass volumes are not typical in his work, pointing out that in the rather gray, northern climate of Dortmund a more closed building would have been inappropriate.

Das Hauptvolumen der Stadt- und Landesbibliothek Dortmund mit einer Gesamtfläche von 14 130 m² ist ein abgestufter Kubus, aus dessen Hauptfassade eine große Halbkreisform hervortritt. Der Eingang befindet sich in der Stumpfzylinderform, die auf Straßenniveau einen Durchmesser von 25,9 m und an ihrem höchsten Punkt von 29,5 m hat. Mario Botta sagt in seinem Erläuterungstext: »Der Entwurf will die Stadt in ihrer Front zum Bahnhofsausgang verdichten. Deshalb teilt sich der Neubau in zwei deutlich voneinander unterscheidbare Teile: in ein massives, streng reduziertes lineares Steinvolumen, das die Außenmauer und Vorderseite definiert, und einen Kegelstumpf aus Glas, der Lesesaal und Freizeitbereiche aufnimmt.« Der Architekt konstatiert selbst, daß große Glasvolumen für sein Werk untypisch seien, setzt aber hinzu, daß ein Bau von größerer Geschlossenheit für die Stadt Dortmund mit ihrem häufig grauen Himmel nicht angemessen gewesen wäre.

Caractérisée par un volume principal rectangulaire en escalier et une forme semicirculaire importante émergeant de sa façade, la bibliothèque municipale offre 14 130 m² de surface utile. L'entrée est située dans le cône tronqué de 25,9 m de rayon à la base et de 29,5 au sommet. Mario Botta précise que « le projet se propose de renforcer le front urbain à la sortie de la gare. C'est pourquoi le nouveau bâtiment est divisé en deux parties distinctes : un volume austère et massif de pierre rouge qui complète ce front, et un cône de verre tronqué qui se détache de l'alignement et sert de salle de lecture et de zone de détente. » Si les grands volumes vitrés ne sont pas typiques de son travail, l'architecte fait remarquer que dans le climat septentrional et la lumière grise de la Ruhr, un bâtiment fermé aurait semblé peu approprié.

Always concerned by the urban aspect of his buildings, Mario Botta here signals his presence in the rounded volume seen in the sketch to the left, and the interior view to the right. The austere rear volume with its typical rows of narrow rectangular windows is contrasted with the glass shape in the foreground (pp. 148/149) – an unusual element in Mario Botta's work.

Botta ist die Präsenz seiner Bauten im städtischen Kontext wichtig, deshalb betont er sie bei diesem Bibliotheksbau durch das vorgelagerte, halbkreisförmige, verglaste Volumen. Der hinter diesem liegende rechtwinklige Gebäudeteil (S. 148/149) weist die für Bottas Architektur typischen Reihen schmaler Fensteröffnungen auf. Der vollverglaste Vorbau stellt in Bottas Werk eine Seltenheit dar.

Toujours sensible à l'intégration urbaine de ses réalisations, Mario Botta signale néanmoins la présence de la bibliothèque par le volume arrondi du croquis de gauche, que l'on retrouve réalisé dans la photo de droite. Le volume arrière (pp. 148/149), aux rangées typiques d'austères fenêtres rectangulaires, vient en contrepoint de la forme vitrée du premier plan, solution rare chez Botta.

Although the shape of the reading rooms is not
a surprise in the Botta œuvre, the fact that it is
entirely clad in glass is. The night view to the right
emphasizes the transparency of the building,
structured by the V-shaped braces.

Oben: Blick in den Zugangsbereich zum
Lesesaal. Rechts unten: Bei Dunkelheit wird das
Lesesaalgebäude nicht nur von innen erhellt,
sondern auch mittels in den Boden eingelassener
Scheinwerfer von außen angestrahlt, so daß die
Zickzacklinien der konstruktiven Verglasung deut-
lich hervortreten.

Si la forme de la salle de lecture ne surprend
pas chez Botta, il n'en va pas de même du matériau utilisé, le verre. La vue nocturne (à droite)
met en valeur la transparence du bâtiment et de
la structure porteuse en zigzag du mur-rideau.

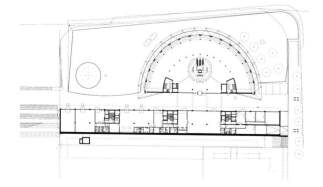

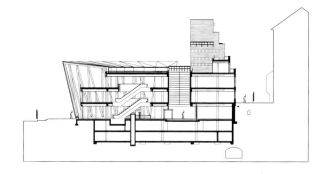

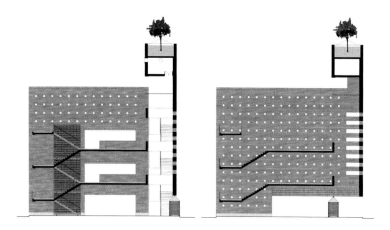

"Cumbre de las Americas" Monument
Santa Cruz de la Sierra, Bolivia, 1996

This monument, says Mario Botta, "was built to mark the 'summit on sustainable growth' (Cumbre sobre Desarrollo Sostenible) that was inaugurated in Santa Cruz on December 6, 1996. The main idea of the project was to design an entrance area for an existing park." Standing 22 meters high, the two structures are clad in red brick. The almost detached "heads" on the buildings, each with porthole "eyes," give an anthropomorphic aspect to the project, which may recall Mayan guardian figures: for example, the sculptures of Chac Mool at Chichén Itzá, Yucatan. It was intended that the portholes be "connected" by a laser beam visible at night. An interesting detail is that these buildings were erected in just three months by teams of 400 workers on three daily shifts. The project was carried out in collaboration with the local architect Luis Fernandez de Cordova.

Das Denkmal »Cumbre de las Americas« wurde errichtet, um – so Botta – »das ›Gipfeltreffen über nachhaltige Entwicklung‹ (Cumbre sobre Desarrollo Sostenible) zu würdigen, das am 6. Dezember 1996 in Santa Cruz eröffnet wurde. Hauptanliegen des baulichen Projekts war, einen Eingangsbereich zu einem bestehenden Park zu schaffen.« Die beiden Baukörper sind 22 m hoch und mit rotem Ziegelstein-Mauerwerk verkleidet. Ihre beinahe losgelösten, mit »Bullaugen« versehenen »Kopfteile« verleihen dem Werk menschlich anmutende Züge und erinnern gewissermaßen an Wächtergestalten der Maya, zum Beispiel die Chac-Mool-Figuren in Chichén Itzá, Yucatán. Die »Bullaugen« sollten nachts durch einen Laserstrahl miteinander »verbunden« werden. In nur drei Monaten wurde das Denkmal von 400 Arbeitern erbaut, die täglich in drei Schichten zu Werk gingen. Das Projekt wurde in Zusammenarbeit mit dem ortsansässigen Architekten Luis Fernandez de Cordova realisiert.

« Ce monument », raconte Mario Botta, « a été construit à l'occasion du ‹ sommet sur la croissance maîtrisée › (Cumbre sobre Desarrollo Sostenible), tenu à Santa Cruz, Bolivie, le 6 décembre 1996. L'idée principale était de concevoir une zone d'entrée pour un parc existant. » De 22 m de haut, les deux bâtiments sont plaqués de brique rouge. Les deux « têtes » presque détachées, chacune dotée d'un œil-de-bœuf, donnent un aspect anthropomorphique à ce projet, qui peut rappeler certaines images de guerriers mayas, comme les sculptures de Chac Mool à Chichén Itzá. Les deux œils-de-bœuf devaient être reliés la nuit par un rayon laser. Ces deux constructions ont été érigées en trois mois seulement, par des équipes de 400 ouvriers pratiquant les 3 x 8. Le projet a été mené à bien en collaboration avec l'architecte bolivien, Luis Fernandez de Cordova.

Recalling the trees he placed on the "Ransila 1" and Evry buildings, Mario Botta again makes the same symbolic gesture (placing nature above the built work). These structures are all the more interesting in that they are essentially symbolic in nature and function.

Botta setzt auch hier (wie in Evry) die Symbolik des Baumes auf einem Gebäude ein: Die Natur steht über der gebauten Umwelt. Diese Bauten sind von daher so interessant, als sie ihrem Charakter und ihrer Funktion nach symbolhaft wirken.

Rappel des arbres de l'immeuble « Ransila 1» et de la cathédrale d'Evry, cet arbre symbolique introduit la nature, hiérarchiquement supérieure à l'œuvre construite.

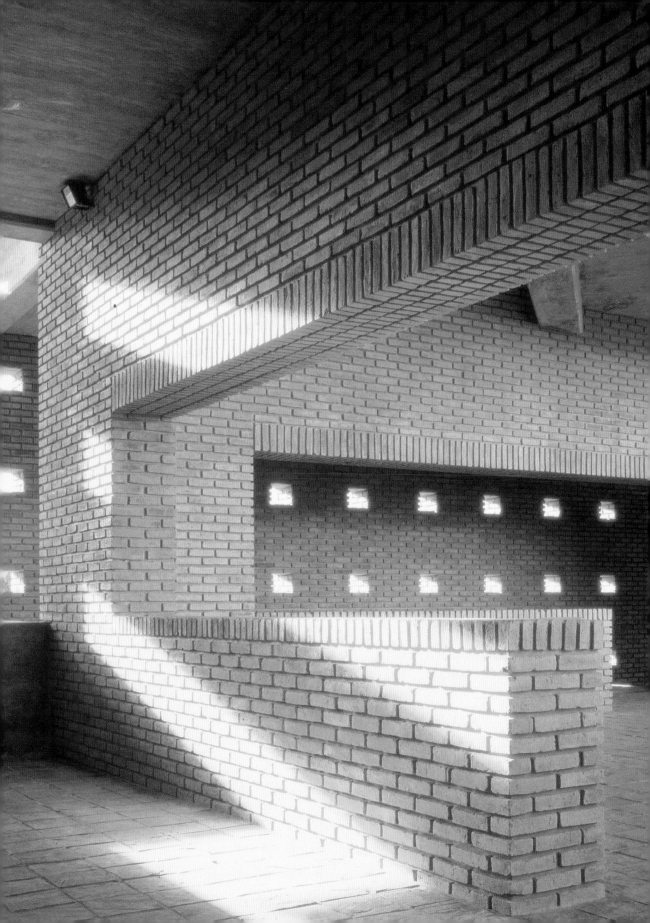

Here, as on a number of other occasions, Mario
Botta makes a passing reference to a figurative
model – in this instance in the form of reclining
Mayan sculptures. The notion of a city gate is
also present.

Auch hier spielt Mario Botta auf figürliche
Vorbilder an, auf die Wächtergestalten der Maya.
Möglicherweise spielte beim Entwurf auch der
Gedanke an ein Stadttor eine Rolle.

Ici, comme dans de nombreuses autres occasions, Mario Botta fait une référence discrète
à un modèle figuratif, en l'espèce des sculptures
couchées mayas. Le concept de porte de ville n'est
également pas loin.

"Cumbre de las Americas" Monument, Santa Cruz de la Sierra 155

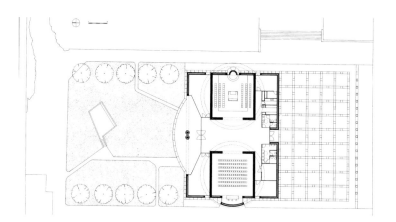

The Cymbalista Synagogue and Jewish Heritage Center
Tel Aviv, Israel, 1996–1998

Located in the grounds of Tel Aviv University, this structure could not be strictly religious since the University is lay. This explains, to some extent, the "bicephalic" nature of the design, with one volume housing a synagogue, and the other, almost identical one containing a study center. Proposed by Mario Botta, this solution won the support of university officials as well as that of the sponsor of the project, Norbert Cymbalista. A suspended roof system brings ample natural overhead light into both spaces, which rise to a height of 10.5 meters and taper upwards and outwards from the level of the base. Mario Botta has written that "the use of the same plastic, formal, spatial and daylighting features in the two volumes reflects a symbolic choice expressing the twofold provision of a religious and secular space for the spiritual and cultural activities of contemporary students."

Der Komplex auf dem Gelände der Universität von Tel Aviv ist nicht ausschließlich für religiöse Zwecke bestimmt, da die Hochschule konfessionell unabhängig ist. Daraus erklärt sich bis zu einem gewissen Grad auch die »zweiköpfige« Struktur des Entwurfs: Der eine Baukörper beherbergt die Cymbalista-Synagoge, der andere, fast identische, ein Museum und das Zentrum für Judaica-Studien, das Jewish Heritage Center. Der Vorschlag Mario Bottas fand die Zustimmung der Universität sowie des Sponsors, Norbert Cymbalista. Eine Hängedachkonstruktion läßt ausreichend Tageslicht in die beiden Innenbereiche einfallen. Beide würfelförmigen Innenräume (Kantenlänge 10,5 m) weiten sich nach oben zu Zylindern mit 15 m Durchmesser. In seinem Erläuterungstext schreibt Botta: »Die Entsprechungen in der plastischen Ausformung, in den räumlichen Verhältnissen und die natürliche Belichtung in beiden Volumen reflektieren eine symbolische Auswahl: ein zweifaches Angebot an Räumen – sakral und säkular – für die spirituellen sowie kulturellen Aktivitäten der Studenten von heute.«

Implanté dans l'enceinte de l'université de Tel Aviv, cette structure ne pouvait être strictement religieuse puisque cet établissement universitaire est laïque. Ceci explique, dans une certaine mesure, la nature bicéphale du projet, un volume abritant une synagogue et l'autre, presque identique, un centre d'étude. Cette solution proposée par Mario Botta a remporté l'agrément des responsables de l'université comme celui du mécène, Norbert Cymbalista. Un système de toits suspendus délivre une généreuse lumière naturelle dans les deux espaces et s'élève à une hauteur de 10,5 m en se rétrécissant vers le haut et vers l'extérieur à partir de sa base. Mario Botta a écrit que « l'utilisation des mêmes caractéristiques plastiques, formelles, spatiales et d'éclairage naturel dans les deux volumes reflète un choix symbolique qui exprime ce que peut apporter un espace séculier et religieux pour les activités spirituelles et culturelles des étudiants d'aujourd'hui. »

Again fundamentally symmetrical, this design differs from many other Botta buildings both in its choice of cladding materials and in its unusual "bicephalic" design intended to overcome university opposition to a purely religious building in a non-religious institution.

Auch dieses Gebäude ist streng symmetrisch aufgebaut, es unterscheidet sich aber sowohl durch seine Materialien als auch die ungewöhnliche »zweiköpfige« Gestalt von Bottas anderen Werken.

Toujours aussi symétrique, ce projet diffère cependant de beaucoup d'autres de l'architecte tant par le choix de ses matériaux de parement que dans son organisation « bicéphale » voulue pour dépasser la problématique d'un bâtiment purement religieux dans une institution laïque.

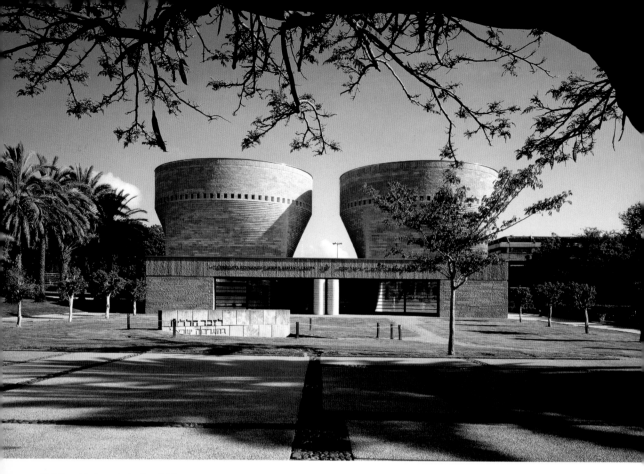

Botta's work is strongest when it maintains a rapport with the relatively simple geometric forms he has always preferred. The skylighting device of a square inscribed in a circle (right) is typical of the power of which he is capable.

Bottas Bauten besitzen die stärkste Wirkung, wenn sie mit den einfachen geometrischen Formen arbeiten, die der Architekt immer bevorzugt hat. Die Deckengestaltung mit Oberlichtern – ein Quadrat im Kreis (rechts) – ist typisch für seine Kreativität und Ausdruckskraft.

L'œuvre de Botta atteint à son sommet lorsqu'elle maintient un rapport avec les formes géométriques simples qu'il préfère depuis toujours. Le dessin de la verrière – un carré inscrit dans un cercle (à droite) – est typique des effets spectaculaires dont il est capable.

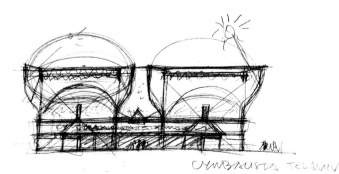

158 **The Cymbalista Synagogue and Jewish Heritage Center**, Tel Aviv

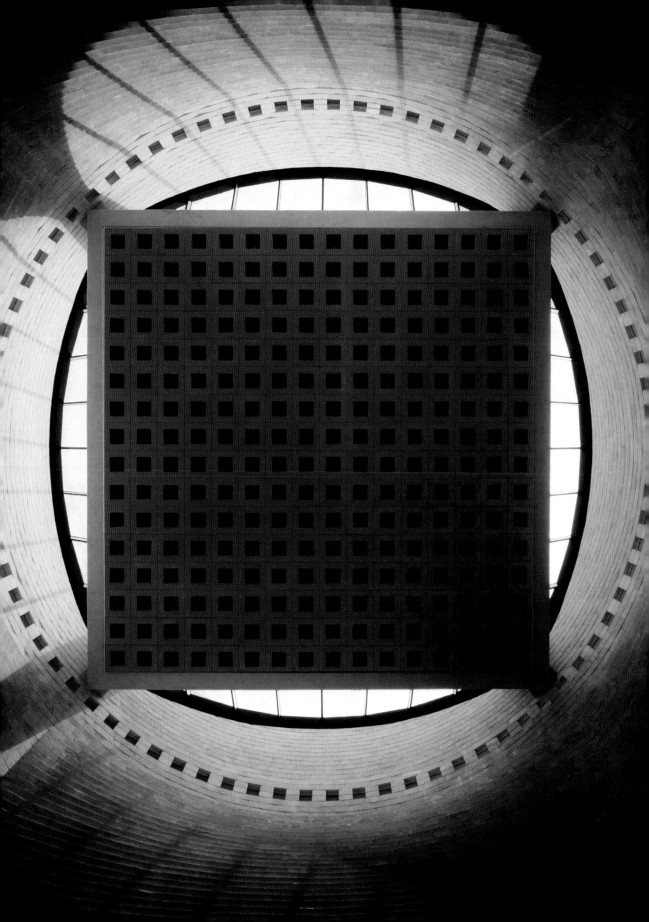

Museum of Modern and Contemporary Art and Cultural Center

Rovereto, Trento, Italy, 1993–2002

This 20,800 m² facility is one of Mario Botta's most important projects. The architect used an existing narrow street set between two historic buildings, the Palazzo Alberti and the Palazzo dell'Annona as the axis for the entry passage to this large complex. Mario Botta speaks in terms of an "umbilical cord" linking the historic city to the new museum when he explains this axial passageway. Although as usual not specifically anthropomorphic, the round central partially covered piazza with a diameter of 40 meters does have a womb-like connotation, confirmed by Botta's own recourse to the vocabulary of childbirth. Aside from this important round inner courtyard, the design evolves from the superimposition of two rectangular forms. Measuring ninety by seventy-five meters overall, the structure is clad in Pietra Dorata slabs, and was commissioned by the city of Rovereto and the Trento region.

Diese Museumsanlage mit 20 800 m² Nutzfläche ist eines von Mario Bottas bedeutendsten Projekten. Der Architekt nutzte eine Gasse zwischen zwei historischen Bauten – dem Palazzo Alberti und dem Palazzo dell'Annona – als Zugangsweg zum großen Gebäudekomplex. Mario Botta bezeichnet diese Zugangsachse als »Nabelschnur« zwischen der Altstadt und dem neuen Museum. Das zentrale, teilweise überdachte Atrium (Durchmesser: 40 m) ist zwar, wie bei Botta üblich, nicht direkt anthropomorph ausgebildet, es schwingt hier aber die Konnotation einer Gebärmutter mit, was zu Bottas Metapher der Nabelschnur paßt. Bis auf dieses große, runde Atrium ergibt sich die insgesamt 90 x 75 m umfassende Baugestalt aus der Überlagerung zweier rechteckiger Massen. Der von der Stadt Rovereto und der Provinz Trento in Auftrag gegebene Museumsbau ist mit Marmor (pietra dorata) verkleidet.

Cet ensemble de 20 800 m², commandé par la ville de Rovereto et la région de Trente, est l'une des plus importantes réalisations de Mario Botta. Une rue étroite située entre deux bâtiments historiques, le Palazzo Alberti et le Palazzo dell'Annona, constitue l'axe du passage d'entrée. Mario Botta évoque à son sujet l'idée d'un « cordon ombilical » entre la vieille ville et le nouveau musée. Bien qu'elle ne soit pas spécifiquement anthropomorphique, la place centrale ronde en partie couverte, d'un diamètre de 40 mètres, fait penser à une matrice, ce que confirme le vocabulaire centré sur la naissance qu'utilise l'architecte. En dehors de cette importante cour intérieure circulaire, le projet se développe à partir de la superposition de deux formes rectangulaires. Mesurant 90 x 75 mètres, le bâtiment est habillé de dalles de pietra dorata.

In a sense similar to a womb, the inner courtyard of the Museum is nonetheless filled with light. The overall volume of the Museum, some 140,000 m³ attests to the generosity of the space. Above, a sketch by Mario Botta representing the courtyard and skylight.

Obwohl er in gewisser Weise wie ein Schutzraum für werdendes Leben im Mutterleib anmutet, wird der Innenhof des Museums von Tageslicht durchflutet. Das Gesamtvolumen von rund 140 000 m³ verrät die Großzügigkeit seines Raumangebots. Oben: Skizze des Innenhofs und des Oberlichts von Mario Botta.

D'une certaine façon similaire à une matrice, la cour intérieure n'en est pas moins baignée de lumière. Le volume global du musée, 140 000 m³, est particulièrement généreux. En haut, croquis de Mario Botta représentant la cour et la verrière.

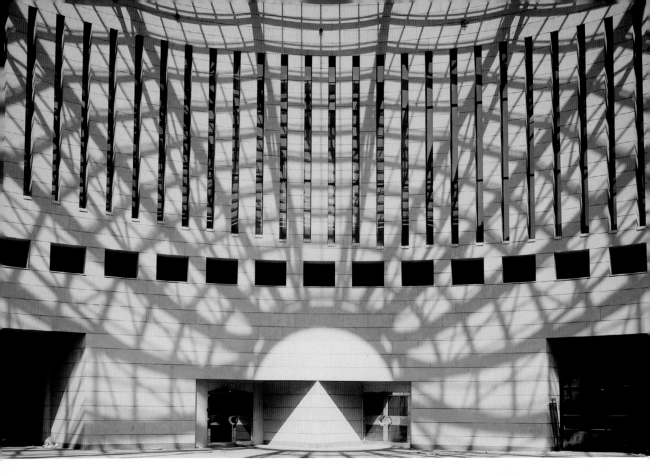

Botta has carefully thought out the transition from the outside world of the city to the inner sanctum of the Museum. A site plan and an image looking from the courtyard toward the city on the right make this relationship clear.

Botta stellte gründliche Überlegungen zur Gestaltung des Übergangs vom städtischen Außenraum in das "Sanktuarium" des Museumsinnern an. Ein Grundrißplan und der Blick vom Hof zur Stadt (rechts) zeigt die Beziehung zwischen beiden.

Botta a aménagé avec soin la transition entre le monde extérieur, la ville, et celui du musée, le sanctuaire. Un plan du site et une image prise de la cour vers la ville (à droite) montrent cette relation.

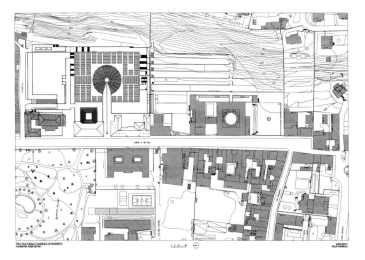

Le Stanze dell'Arte. Figure e immagini del XX secolo

The large exhibition rooms are located on the first level, while the second floor houses smaller exhibition areas. Access to the galleries on the two upper floors runs around the central courtyard, while staircases occupy the corners of the square that circumscribes the round heart of the complex.

Die großen Ausstellungsgalerien sind auf der ersten Ebene untergebracht, während die zweite die kleineren Galerien umfaßt. Der Zugang zu den beiden oberen Ausstellungsetagen erfolgt rund um den Innenhof und über Treppenhäuser in den Ecken des Quadrats, das den runden Kern des Gebäudes umschließt.

Les grandes salles d'exposition sont implantées au rez-de-chaussée, tandis que l'étage accueille des espaces moins vastes. L'accès aux galeries des deux étages supérieurs court autour du vide central, et les escaliers sont reportés aux angles du plan en carré qui entoure le cœur cylindrique du complexe.

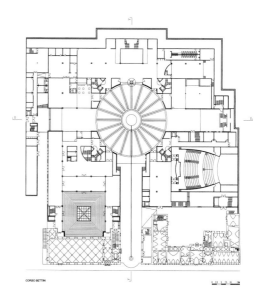

CORSO BETTINI

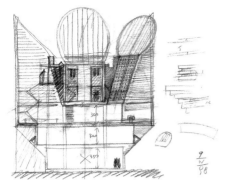

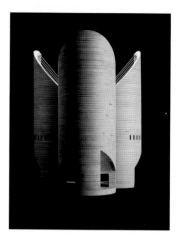

Church at Malpensa Airport
Milan, Italy, 1998 (Project)

The site for this church is an angle formed by an elevated access ramp for the airport and the departure buildings. Mario Botta compares the plan of the structure to a "clover." A triangular 14.5-meter high volume forms the center of the base, with three vertically sectioned cylinders above. At the upper level (height of 14.5 meters) a bridge for pedestrians and a 75-square meter square form the entrance area. Four levels containing the chapel, offices, a multi-use room and technical spaces are located beneath the entrance area. The total covered area is 364 square meters. The chapel located midway up the volume (height of 10.6 meters) covers an area of 271 square meters. The total height of the building is 31 meters, and the entire plan is contained within a 24.6-meter circle. The load-bearing structure is made of reinforced concrete, and exterior façades and a part of the interior walls are covered in red Verona stone (Pietra Rossa di Verona).

Eine aufgeständerte Zufahrtsrampe zu den Gebäuden des Mailänder Flughafens ist das »Grundstück« für diese Kapelle. Mario Botta vergleicht den Grundriß mit einem Kleeblatt. Ein dreieckiger, 14,5 m hoher Baukörper bildet den Kern des Sockelgeschosses, über dem sich drei vertikal gegliederte Zylinder erheben. Auf der oberen Ebene (14,5 m Höhe) formen eine Fußgängerbrücke und ein 75 m² umfassender Vorplatz den Eingangsbereich. Vier Geschosse bieten Platz für den Kapellenraum, Büros, einen Mehrzwecksaal und Räume für die Haustechnik unterhalb des Eingangsbereichs. Die gesamte Grundfläche beträgt 364 m². Der Kapellenraum liegt etwa auf halber Höhe des insgesamt 31 m hohen Bauwerks und hat eine Fläche von 271 m². Der Grundriß ist ein Kreis von 24,6 m Durchmesser. Das Tragwerk besteht aus Stahlbeton, die Außenfassaden und ein Teil der Innenwände sind mit Platten aus rotem Veroneser Marmor verkleidet.

La chapelle s'élève entre une rampe d'accès et le bâtiment des départs de l'aéroport. Mario Botta en compare le plan à un « trèfle ». Un volume triangulaire de 14,5 m de haut forme le centre du socle sur lequel viennent se greffer trois cylindres coupés dans le sens de la hauteur. Au niveau supérieur (14,5 m de hauteur) une passerelle et une dalle carrée de 75 m² constituent l'entrée. Les quatre niveaux contiennent la chapelle, des bureaux, une salle polyvalente, et des espaces techniques logés sous l'entrée. La surface utile totale est de 364 m². La chapelle implantée vers la mi-hauteur (10,6 m de hauteur) mesure 271 m² de surface. La hauteur totale du bâtiment est de 31 m, et l'emprise au sol est contenue dans un cercle de 24,6 m de diamètre. La structure porteuse est en béton armé tandis que les façades et une partie des murs intérieurs sont recouverts de pierre de Vérone rouge (pietra rossa di Verona).

The truncated cylinder often employed by the architect is here multiplied by three, and elongated upwards. Despite the relatively small size of the church, it retains the monumentality often inscribed in Mario Botta's architecture.

In Malpensa hat Botta die von ihm häufig verwendete Form des Stumpfzylinders zum Kleeblatt verdreifacht und in die Höhe gestreckt. Obwohl sie relativ klein ist, wirkt die Kapelle doch ebenso »monumental« wie viele andere Bauten Bottas.

La forme en cylindre tronqué souvent utilisée par l'architecte est ici multipliée par trois, et étirée vers le haut. En dépit de sa taille relativement réduite, cette église conserve la monumentalité caractéristique de l'architecture de Mario Botta.

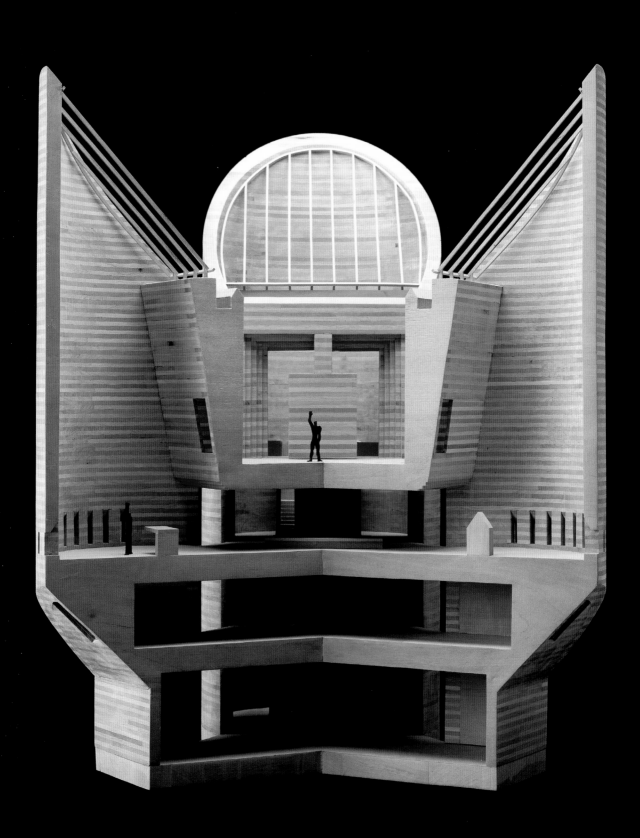

"Noah's Ark", Sculpture Garden, with Niki de Saint Phalle
Jerusalem, Israel, 1995–2001

Located at the Jerusalem Zoo, this project was commissioned by the City of Jerusalem and the Jerusalem Foundation. It was designed in collaboration with Niki de Saint Phalle, widow of the Swiss artist Jean Tinguely and a talented sculptor in her own right. Botta himself best describes this structure whose underground built volume is 2,700 m³. "When Niki de Saint Phalle asked me to collaborate on building Noah's Ark to be inserted in a park, I enthusiastically accepted the invitation. It led me to think of a negative sign – almost as if the area were present as a petrified impression left as a sediment in the green plane of the park. Built of Jerusalem stone, the structure is part of a play facility for children. Outside, they find highly colored animal sculptures modeled by Niki de Saint Phalle. The underground spaces of the Ark and the internal cavities of the sculptures create a suitably reduced scale for which the project was conceived."

Die im Jerusalemer Zoo geschaffene Anlage wurde von der Stadt Jerusalem und der Jerusalem-Stiftung gemeinsam in Auftrag gegeben und entstand in Zusammenarbeit mit der Bildhauerin Niki de Saint Phalle, der Witwe des schweizerischen Künstlers Jean Tinguely. Botta beschreibt die unter Bodenniveau angelegte »Arche« mit ihrem Gesamtvolumen von 2 700 m³ so: »Als Niki de Saint Phalle mich fragte, ob ich mit ihr eine Arche Noah für einen Park bauen würde, habe ich begeistert zugesagt. Ich dachte an ein Negativzeichen: an ein Gelände, das sozusagen einen fossilen Abdruck im Sediment der grünen Parkfläche darstellt. Die Anlage aus Jerusalemer Stein gehört zu einem Kinderspielplatz. Darum herum finden die Kinder fröhliche, bunte Tierplastiken von Niki de Saint Phalle. Die unterirdischen Räume der Arche und die Hohlräume in den Skulpturen bieten die den Kindern angemessenen räumlichen Dimensionen.«

Situé dans le zoo de Jérusalem, ce projet est une commande de la ville et de la Jerusalem Foundation. Il a été conçu en collaboration avec Niki de Saint Phalle, épouse de Jean Tinguely, et elle-même sculpteur de talent. Botta décrit ainsi cette construction dont le volume souterrain représente 2 700 m³ : « Lorsque Niki de Saint Phalle m'a demandé de collaborer à cette arche de Noé dans un parc, j'ai accepté avec enthousiasme. J'ai pensé à un signe négatif – un peu comme si la zone était l'impression pétrifiée laissée par un sédiment dans le plan de verdure du parc. Construite en pierre de Jérusalem, l'arche fait partie d'un équipement de jeux pour les enfants. À l'extérieur, ils découvrent les animaux aux couleurs éclatantes de Niki de Saint-Phalle. Les volumes souterrains de l'arche et les cavités internes des sculptures déterminent une échelle réduite adaptée à ceux pour qui le projet a été conçu. »

The brightly colored sculptures of Niki de Saint Phalle animate the green areas and the underground gallery designed by Mario Botta. A site sketch, above, shows the location of the architectural and sculptural elements of the composition.

Die bunten Skulpturen von Niki de Saint Phalle beleben die Grünflächen und die von Mario Botta geschaffene unterirdische Ausstellungsgalerie. Eine Grundriß-Skizze (oben) zeigt die Anordnung der architektonischen und plastischen Elemente der Anlage.

Les sculptures de couleurs vives par Niki de Saint Phalle animent les pelouses et la galerie souterraine conçue par Mario Botta. Un croquis du site, ci-dessus, montre l'implantation des éléments architecturaux et sculpturaux de la composition.

Headquarters of the National Bank of Greece
Athens, Greece, 1999–2001

Set on the corner of Sofokleou and Eolou Streets from which the Acropolis is visible, this bank headquarters is in the historic center of Athens. It is located near registered buildings, the bank's main building, the Stock Exchange and the Mela Mansion. The architect's task was complicated by the discovery on-site of the archeological remains of Acharniki Street, and the decision to render the ground floor as transparent as possible in this context. A large void was created to make the moat of an ancient wall, 9 meters below, visible. Metal bridges and glass floors on the ground floor assure that the archeological findings can be seen in this six-story structure with four basements that extend under what remains of the former Acharniki Street. Sandstone is used for exterior cladding and major structural elements inside. Black matte granite on the floors and light-colored wood on walls and ceilings complete the scheme.

Dieses Bankgebäude Ecke Sofokleou- und Eolou-Straße in der Altstadt von Athen, ganz in der Nähe denkmalgeschützter Bauten (Hauptniederlassung der Bank, Börse und Villa Mela) bietet Ausblick auf die Akropolis. Die Aufgabe des Architekten wurde erschwert durch die archäologischen Reste der einstigen Acharniki-Straße und die Vorgabe, das Erdgeschoß der Bankzentrale in diesem Zusammenhang so transparent wie möglich zu gestalten. Er schuf deshalb einen großen, leeren Raum, um den 9 m unter Planum freigelegten antiken Wall sichtbar zu machen. Metallbrücken und Glasböden sorgen dafür, daß die archäologischen Stätten von diesem sechsgeschossigen Hochbau nicht verdeckt werden, der zusätzlich vier Tiefgeschosse unter der einstigen Acharniki-Straße umfaßt. Die Fassadenverkleidung und wesentliche tragende Elemente im Innern bestehen aus Sandstein. Mattschwarze Granitböden sowie helles Holz an Wänden und Decken vervollständigen die Material- und Farbenpalette.

Ce siège de banque, d'où l'on peut apercevoir l'Acropole, se dresse dans le centre historique d'Athènes, à l'angle des rues Sofokleou et Eolou, à proximité de bâtiments classés, dont le siège principal de la banque, la bourse et la résidence Mela. La tâche de l'architecte a été rendue plus difficile par la découverte de vestiges archéologiques de la rue Acharniki, ce qui explique la décision de rendre le rez-de-chaussée aussi transparent que possible. Un large vide a été aménagé pour permettre de voir le fossé d'un ancien rempart, à neuf mètres de profondeur, tandis que des passerelles métalliques et des sols de verre au rez-de-chaussée laissent entrevoir certains vestiges. Les façades et les principaux éléments structurels internes de cet immeuble de dix niveaux, dont quatre en sous-sol, sont habillés de grès. Les sols sont recouverts de granit noir mat et les plafonds et les murs sont pour la plupart revêtus d'un bois clair.

Although its modern lines are not directly related either to the Classical tradition of Greece, nor to the Neo-Classic aspect of neighboring buildings, Botta's strong notched façade, revealing the underlying archeological site, is certainly not incongruous in modern Athens.

Die modernen Linien von Bottas ausdrucksstarker eingekerbter Fassade, die auf die dahinter liegende archäologische Fundstätte hinweist, besitzt zwar keine direkten Bezüge zur klassischen Antike Griechenlands oder zum Neoklassizismus der Nachbarbauten, wirkt aber dennoch nicht fehl am Platz im heutigen Athen.

Bien que sa modernité soit sans lien avec la tradition classique grecque ou le néoclassicisme des bâtiments environnants, cette façade aux puissantes découpes qui révèlent un site architectural jusqu'alors invisible, ne semble pas vraiment incongrue dans l'Athènes moderne.

SECTION

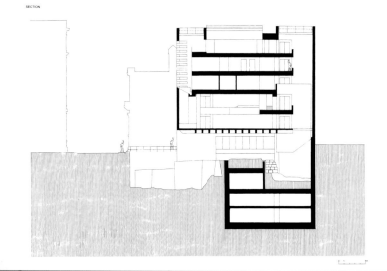

A section (left) and a photo show how the architect has resolved the problem of the preservation of the archeological site, while still providing four basements.

Ein Schnitt (links) und ein Foto verdeutlichen, wie der Architekt die Aufgabe gelöst hat, die archäologische Grabung zu erhalten und zugleich vier Kellergeschosse zu schaffen.

La coupe (à gauche) et une photo montrent comment l'architecte a résolu le problème de la préservation d'un site archéologique, tout en aménageant quatre niveaux de sous-sols.

A strong contrast emerges between the apparently blank façades of a good part of the structure and the presence of light inside. Both the heat of Athens and the banking function of the structure plead in favor of the rather massive stone-clad design.

Ein starker Gegensatz tut sich auf zwischen den zum größten Teil scheinbar durchgehend geschlossenen Fassaden und der Belichtung der Innenräume. Sowohl die sommerliche Hitze Athens als auch die Bankfunktion des Gebäudes begünstigten die Entwurfsentscheidung für einen relativ massiven, mit Stein verkleideten Bau.

Un puissant contraste se crée entre les façades apparemment aveugles d'une grande partie du bâtiment et la présence intérieure de la lumière. La chaleur du climat athénien et les fonctions bancaires plaidaient pour cette conception assez massive et habillée de pierre.

Dürrenmatt Center
Neuchâtel, Switzerland, 1992/97–2000

This small museum houses a collection of drawings by the Swiss novelist and playwright Friedrich Dürrenmatt. Mario Botta decided that the museum should be placed next to the author's home. A rounded, partially buried "tower" with a radius of 28.4 meters was created with double-height galleries situated below a platform. The volume of the structure is 4,700 m3. Approaching from the rear, the visitor enters on a bridge that forms "an implied axis inside the tower, an axis also indicated by the glass surface on one side and the round glass on the other side of the walls." The tower's walls clad in gray 10 cm thick slate. Ample daylight enters the exhibition spaces from long openings. Gray slate is also used for the floors of the museum. Dürrenmatt's library and a small cafeteria are located in the original house. As in other cases, Mario Botta works with an existing building and adds to it partially by digging below ground. Solidity too is a constant quality of Botta's architecture, and here it expresses the strengths of the author whose work is celebrated in Neuchâtel.

Dieses kleine Museum bewahrt eine Sammlung von Zeichnungen des schweizerischen Schriftstellers und Dramatikers Friedrich Dürrenmatt auf. Mario Botta entschied, das Museum neben dem Wohnhaus des Autors zu errichten. Entstanden ist ein teilweise in den Boden eingelassener runder »Turm« mit einem Durchmesser von 28,4 m und sehr hohen Ausstellungsräumen unterhalb einer Terrasse. Das Bauvolumen umfasst 4 700 m3. Besucher betreten den Bau von der Rückseite über eine Brücke, die sich in einer »unsichtbaren Achse im Turm fortsetzt und von der Glasfläche auf der einen und dem runden Glas auf der anderen Seite der Wände angedeutet wird«. Die Außenmauern sind mit 10 cm dicken Schieferplatten verkleidet. Tageslicht durchflutet die Räume durch lange Fensteröffnungen. Auch die Böden des Museums sind mit Schieferplatten belegt. Dürrenmatts Bibliothek und ein kleines Café sind in seinem Wohnhaus untergebracht. Massivität ist eine Konstante in Bottas Schaffen, hier steht sie für die Kraft von Dürrenmatts Werk.

Mario Botta a décidé d'implanter près de la maison de l'écrivain ce musée qui abrite une collection de dessins du romancier et auteur dramatique suisse Friedrich Dürrenmatt. Une « tour » cylindrique, en partie enfouie, de 28,4 mètres de rayon contient des galeries de grande hauteur situées sous une plate-forme. Le volume total s'élève à 4 700 m3. Pénétrant par l'arrière du bâtiment, le visiteur emprunte une passerelle qui forme « un axe à l'intérieur de la tour, axe confirmé par les parois de verres d'un côté et les panneaux de verre incurvé sur l'autre face des murs ». Les murs de la tour et les sols sont habillés d'ardoise de 10 centimètres d'épaisseur. La lumière naturelle abondante, qui arrive des longues ouvertures, éclaire les espaces d'exposition. La bibliothèque de Dürrenmatt et une petite cafétéria ont été aménagées dans la maison d'origine. Comme dans d'autres interventions sur des bâtiments existants, Mario Botta enterre en partie son apport. La solidité massive, une constante de son œuvre, exprime ici la puissance de l'œuvre de Dürrenmatt.

The architect's sketch, above, shows the relation between the existing house and the new spaces. To the right, natural light penetrates the new gallery area.

Die Skizze des Architekten (oben) verdeutlicht die Beziehung zwischen dem alten Wohnhaus und dem Neubau. Rechts: Tageslicht durchdringt die neuen Ausstellungsräume.

Le croquis de l'architecte, ci-dessus, montre la relation entre la maison existante et les nouveaux volumes. À droite, la lumière naturelle inonde la nouvelle galerie.

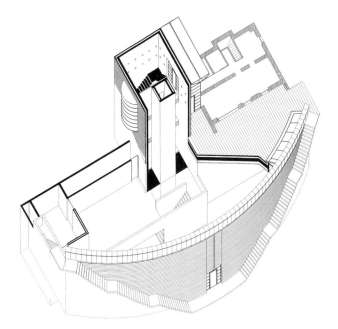

An axonometric drawing and the photo below
emphasize the symmetrical and almost funerary
power of Botta's concept.
   Axonometrie und Foto betonen die Symmetrie und fast sepulkrale Würde von Bottas Bau.
   Le dessin axonométrique et la photo ci-dessous mettent en valeur la force symétrique, presque funéraire, de la conception de Botta.

Overlooking the Lake of Neuchâtel, the Dürrenmatt Center has a lush, green setting. Above, the
curved skylight over the new gallery.

Das Dürrenmatt-Zentrum mit Blick über
den Neuenburger See ist von üppigem Grün
umgeben. Oben: Das gewölbte Oberlicht im
Galerie-Neubau.

Donnant sur le lac de Neuchâtel, le Centre
Dürrenmatt est situé dans un riche cadre de verdure. En haut, la verrière incurvée qui recouvre la
nouvelle galerie.

1959

Single Family House
Morbio Superiore, Ticino, Switzerland

1961

Parish House
Genestrerio, Ticino, Switzerland, 1961–63
(with Tita Carloni)

Parish House, Genestrerio

1965

Single Family House
Stabio, Ticino, Switzerland

Single Family House, Stabio

1966

Chapel in the Monastery of Santa Maria
Bigorio, Ticino, Switzerland
(with Tita Carloni)

Single Family House
Genestrerio, Ticino, Switzerland

1970

Single Family House
Cadenazzo, Ticino, Switzerland, 1970–71

Single Family House, Cadenazzo

1971

Single Family House
Riva San Vitale, Ticino, Switzerland, 1971–73

New Administration Center
Perugia, Italy, competition
(with Luigi Snozzi)

1972

Middle School
Morbio Inferiore, Ticino, Switzerland, 1972–77

1973

Meeting Room at the Monastery of Santa Maria
Bigorio, Ticino, Switzerland

1974

Residential Complex
Rancate, Ticino, Switzerland, competition
(with Luigi Snozzi)

1975

Single Family House
Ligornetto, Ticino, Switzerland, 1975–76

Single Family House
Maggia, Ticino, Switzerland, 1975–77

Single Family House, Ligornetto

1976

Public Gymnasium
Balerna, Ticino, Switzerland, 1976–78

Library of the Capuchin Convent
Lugano, Ticino, Switzerland, 1976–79

Public Gymnasium, Balerna

1977

Extension of the Main Railway Station
Zurich, Switzerland, competition
(with Luigi Snozzi)

Farmhouse
Refurbishment and re-use, Ligrignano, Ticino,
Switzerland, 1977–78

Craft Center
Balerna, Ticino, Switzerland, 1977–79

Farmhouse, Ligrignano

State Bank, Fribourg

Single Family House, Massagno

Single Family House, Stabio

Single Family House, Origlio

Theater, Chambéry

Public Library, Villeurbanne

State Bank
Fribourg, Switzerland, 1977–82

1979

Single Family House
Pregassona, Ticino, Switzerland, 1979–80

Single Family House
Massagno, Ticino, Switzerland, 1979–81

1980

Medical Health Care Home
Agra, Ticino, Switzerland, competition

Redevelopment of a city area
Stuttgart, Germany, competition

Science Center
Berlin, Germany, competition

Single Family House
Viganello, Ticino, Switzerland, 1980–81

Single Family House
Stabio, Ticino, Switzerland, 1980–82

1981

House development
Marne-la-Vallée, France, competition

New Picasso Museum
Guernica, Spain, competition

Single Family House
Origlio, Ticino, Switzerland, 1981–82

Office Building "Ransila 1"
Lugano, Switzerland, 1981–85

1982

Administration Center
Lyon, France, competition

Single Family House
Morbio Superiore, Ticino, Switzerland, 1982–83

**Theater and Cultural Center (Espace Culturel)
André Malraux**
Chambéry, France, 1982–87

Gottardo Bank
Lugano, Switzerland, 1982–88

1984

**Public Library
(Maison du livre, de l'image et du son)**
Villeurbanne, France, 1984–88

Single Family House
Breganzona, Ticino, Switzerland, 1984–88

1985

House Development on Giudecca
Venice, Italy, competition

**Residential Development on the site of
Ex-Venchi Unica**
Turin, Italy
(with Pierpaolo Maggiora, Filippo Barbano,
Mario Deaglio)

ICF Showroom
Design Center, New York

Watari-um Contemporary Art Gallery
Tokyo, Japan, 1985–90

Apartment Building and Architect's Office
Via Ciani, Lugano, Switzerland, 1985–90

Office Building "Ransila 2"
Lugano, Switzerland, 1985–91

Office and Apartment Building for the IBA
Berlin, Germany, 1985–91
(with Bendoraitis, Gurt und Meissner)

Apartment Building and
Architect's Office, Lugano

1986

Multipurpose Development on the area Bicocca
Milan, Italy, competition

**New Galleries for the Thyssen-Bornemisza
Collection**
Lugano-Castagnola, Switzerland, competition

Single Family House
Cavigliano, Ticino, Switzerland, 1986–89

Single Family House
Vacallo, Ticino, Switzerland, 1986–89

Two Family House
Daro-Bellinzona, Ticino, Switzerland, 1986–91

Single Family House, Vacallo

Residences, Offices and Shops
Lugano-Paradiso, Switzerland, 1986–92
(with Gianfranco Agazzi)

Administration Building "Caimato"
Lugano-Cassarate, Switzerland, 1986–93

Union Bank of Switzerland
Basel, Switzerland, 1986–95
(with Burckhardt und Partner)

Church of Saint John the Baptist
Mogno, Valle Maggia, Switzerland, 1986/92–98

Renovation of Piazza della Pace
Parma, Italy, 1986/92–

"Caimato", Lugano-Cassarate

1987

Single Family House
Losone, Ticino, Switzerland, 1987–89

Single Family House
Manno, Ticino, Switzerland, 1987–90

Church of Beato Odorico
Pordenone, Italy, 1987–92
(with Piero Beltrame and Giorgio Raffin)

Family Tomb
Lugano, Switzerland, 1987–92

Single Family House, Manno

Church of San Pietro Apostolo
Sartirana di Merate, Italy, 1987–95
(with Fabiano Redaelli)

Bruxelles Lambert Bank
Geneva, Switzerland, 1987–96

Church, Pordenone

Offices, Bellinzona

Housing Complex, Novazzano

Shopping Halls "S-lunga",
Florence

1988

Renovation of Piazza Cortevecchia
Ferrara, Italy

Redevelopment of the Vallée du Flon
Lausanne, Switzerland (with Vincent Mangeat)

Offices and Residences
Via Nizzola, Bellinzona, Switzerland, 1988–91

Housing Complex
Novazzano, Ticino, Switzerland, 1988–92
(with Ferruccio Robbiani)

Shopping Halls "S-lunga"
Florence, Italy, 1988–92

Cathedral
Evry, France, 1988–95

Residential Complex
Castelfranco Veneto, Italy, 1988–97
(with Luciano and Mario Gemin)

Swisscom Administration Center
Bellinzona, Switzerland, 1988–98

**Museum of Modern and Contemporary Art
and Cultural Center**
Rovereto (Trento), Italy, 1988/93–2002
(with Giulio Andreolli)

1989

Offices, Shops and Theater
Varese, Italy, competition winner
(with Aurelio Galfetti)

**Tent for the Celebration of the 700th Anniversary
of the Swiss Confederation**
Switzerland, 1989–91

Single Family House
Daro-Bellinzona, Ticino, Switzerland, 1989–92

Single Family House
Cologny, Geneva, Switzerland, 1989–93

Showroom and Family House
Zofingen, Switzerland, 1989–93

Single Family House
Montagnola, Ticino, Switzerland, 1989–94

Museum of Modern Art
San Francisco, California, USA, 1989–95
(with Hellmuth, Obata and Kassabaum Inc.)

Administration Building
Pusan, South Korea, 1989–

Single Family House, Montagnola

1990

Offices and Residences
Steinfels-areal, Zurich, Switzerland

Office Building
Rümlang-Zurich, Switzerland

Cultural Center
San Sebastian, Spain, competition

Palazzo del Cinema
Venice, Italy, competition

San Francisco Museum
of Modern Art

Church, Sartirana di Merate

Family Tomb
Lugano, Switzerland, 1990–91

Santa Maria degli Angeli Chapel
Monte Tamaro, Ticino, Switzerland, 1990–96

Chapel, Monte Tamaro

Administration Building
of the Editorial "La Provincia"
Como, Italy, 1990–97
(with Giorgio Orsini)

National Sports Center
Tenero, Ticino, Switzerland, 1990/96–2000

Offices and Residences
Maastricht, Holland, 1990/97–2001

New Casino
Campione d'Italia, 1990/98–
(with Giorgio Orsini)

"La Provincia", Como

1991

Home for Children
Rajsko, Poland, competition

Industrial Building Thermoselect
Fondotoce-Verbania, Italy, 1991

Research Center and Laboratories
Robbiano-Medeglia, Milan, Italy

Extension of the Parliament Building
Berne, Switzerland, competition winner

Industrial Building Thermoselect

Administration Building
Merate, Italy, 1991–97
(with Fabiano Redaelli)

Ten Row Houses
Bernareggio, Italy, 1991–97
(with Bruna Vertemati and Fabiano Redaelli)

Commercial Building, Offices and
Residences Piazzale alla Valle
Mendrisio, Ticino, Switzerland, 1991–98

Ten Row Houses, Bernareggio

1992

New Convention Center
Nara, Japan, competition

Housing
Monte Carasso, Ticino, Switzerland, 1992–96

Commercial and Residential Building
Merate, Italy, 1992–97
(with Bruna Vertemati and Fabiano Redaelli)

Residences Piazzale alla Valle,
Mendrisio

Home for the Elderly
Novazzano, Ticino, Switzerland, 1992–98

Office Building
Taegu, Seoul, South Korea, 1992–2000

Private Library for Werner Oechslin
Einsiedeln, Switzerland, 1992/97–

Home for the Elderly, Novazzano

Friedrich Dürrenmatt Center
Neuchâtel, Switzerland, 1992/97–2000

Single Family House,
Bernareggio

Office Tower, Seoul

Museum Jean Tinguely, Basel

Service Station, Quinto

1993

Single Family House
Bernareggio, Italy, 1993–99
(with Bruna Vertemati and Fabiano Redaelli)

Urban Development on Alexanderplatz
Berlin, Germany, competition

Service Station
Lyon, France, competition
(with Marc Givry)

New Contemporary Art Museum
Zaragoza, Spain, competition winner

Scientific High School
Città della Pieve, Italy, 1993–2003
(with Giorgio Orsini)

Row Houses
Vedü Alto-Merate, Italy

Office Tower
Seoul, South Korea, 1993–2003

Museum Jean Tinguely
Basel, Switzerland, 1993–96

Service Station
Quinto, Ticino, Switzerland, 1993–98

Noise Protection
Viale Galli, Chiasso, Switzerland, 1993–2004

Renovation and Extension of the Querini
Stampalia Foundation
Venic, Italy, 1993–2003

1994

Urban Development
Ex-Appiani, Treviso, Italy
(with Luciano and Mario Gemin)

The Cardiff Bay Opera House
Cardiff, Wales, Great Britain, competition

New Parliament Building
Namur, Belgium, competition winner

1995

Home for the Elderly and Disabled
Trevi, Italy
(with Giorgio Orsini)

Residential and Office Building at Pariser Platz
Berlin, Germany, competition

Open-Air Museum "Noah's Ark"
Jerusalem, Israel, 1995–2001
(with Niki de Saint Phalle)

Museum for Ceramics
Seoul, South Korea

Single Family House
Muzzano, Ticino, Switzerland, 1995–97

Entrance gate to Niki de Saint Phalle's
"Tarot Garden" (Giardino dei Tarocchi)
Garavicchio, Italy, 1995–97
(with Roberto Aureli)

Municipal Library
Dortmund, Germany, 1995–98

Municipal Library, Dortmund

Pier and Landing Stage
Faliro, Thessaloniki, Greece, 1995–

Renovation of Museo Vela
Ligornetto, Ticino, Switzerland, 1995–2001

1996
New Danish National and Provincial Archives
Copenhagen, Denmark, competition

"Cumbre de las Americas" Monument
Santa Cruz de la Sierra, Bolivia
(with Luis Fernandez de Cordova & Roda srl)

Family Tomb
Stabio, Ticino, Switzerland, 1996–97

Reiser Monument
Montparnasse, Paris, France, 1996–97

Industrial Building
Altershausen, Germany, 1996–98

The Cymbalista Synagogue and Jewish Heritage Center
Tel Aviv, Israel, 1996–98

Office Building
New Delhi, India, 1996–2003

Office Building and Hotel
Saint Petersburg, Russia, 1996–

1997
New Philharmony
Luxembourg, competition
(with Alain Leer)

New Museum Würth
Schwäbisch Hall, Germany, competition

Family Tomb
Santa Lucia del Piave, Treviso, Italy

New Apsis for the Santa Maria del Fiore Cathedral
Florence, Italy

New Funicular Stations
Orselina – Cardada, Locarno, Ticino, Switzerland, 1997–2000

New Headquarters of the National Bank
Athens, Greece, 1997–2001, competition
(with Morfo Papanikolaou and Irena Sakellaridou, Salonicco)

Extension of the Bodmer Library
Cologny, Switzerland, 1997–2003

New Cathedral
Fatima, Portugal, 1997/98, competition

1998
Church at Malpensa Airport
Milan, Italy, Project, 1998

Access and Entrance to the Uffizi
Florence, Italy, competition

Headquarters and Embassy of Nordrhein-Westfalen
Berlin, Germany, competition

"Cumbre de las Americas" Monument, Santa Cruz de la Sierra

Cymbalista Synagogue and Jewish Heritage Center, Tel Aviv

New Headquarters of the National Bank, Athens

Church at Malpensa Airport, Milan

Single Family House, Königsberg

San Carlino, Lugano

Harting Office Building, Minden

Tata Consultancy Service Offices, Hyderabad

Sanctuary of Notre Dame de Montara
Magdouche, Lebanon

Single Family House
Königsberg, Germany, 1998–99

New Funicular Stations and Restaurant "Glacier 2000"
Les Diablerets, Switzerland, 1998–2002

Museum for Rupestrian Drawings
Val Camonica, Italy

Belvedere Tower
Moron, Switzerland, 1998–

La Mattonata – Reconstruction and round walk
Assisi, Italy

Redesign of a church façade
Genestrerio, Ticino, Switzerland, 1998–2003

Residences
Deventer, The Netherlands, 1998–

1999
San Carlino
Wood model of Borromini's Church San Carlo alle Quattro Fontane
Lugano, Switzerland, 1999

New Synagogue
Mainz, Germany, competition

Harting Office Building
Minden, Germany, 1999–2001

Hotel and Residences
Schio, Italy

Thermoselect Industrial Building
Giubiasco, Ticino, Switzerland

Vinery *Petra*
Suvereto, Italy, 1999–2003

Tata Consultancy Service Offices
Hyderabad, India

Denver Millenium Marker
Denver, Colorado USA

King Fahd National Library
Riyadh, Saudi Arabia, competition winner

Congress Center and Hotel
Bellinzona, Switzerland

Pedriatic Clinic
Padua, Italy
(with Gabriele Cappellato and Marisa Macchietti)

Residences
Winterthur, Switzerland, competition

Cultural Center
Leuk, Switzerland, 1999–

Urban Masterplan
Monte Carlo, Pincipauté de Monaco

Law Faculty of the University of Trento
Italy, 1999–
(with Emilio Pizzi)

Redesign of the Piazza della Libertà
Travagliato, Italy, 1999–

Golf Club House
Maastricht, The Netherlands

New Opera House
Oslo, Norway, competition

2000
Congress Center
Engelberg, Switzerland

Weekend Houses at Cardada
Locarno, Switzerland, 2000–02

University Library Rostock
Germany, competition

Shopping Mall in Mannheim
Germany

Extension of the National Museum
Zurich, Switzerland, competition

Residences in Ascona
Switzerland

Ambulatory Services
Mendrisio, Switzerland

New Mosque in Strasbourg
France, competition

Hotel in Lazise
Lago di Garda, Italy

Central Bus Terminal
Lugano, Switzerland, 2000–02

Central Bus Terminal, Lugano

Headquarters of the National Insurance Company
Athens, Greece 2000–
(with Morfo Papanikolaou and Irena Sakellaridou, Salonicco)

Bechtler's Museum
Little Italy, Charlotte, North Carolina, 2000–04

Residences
Zermatt, Switzerland

2001
Residences
Haarlemmermeer, The Netherlands

Church of Santo Volto
Turin, Italy, 2001–

Church of Santo Volto, Turin

Urban Development
Arcore, Italy

Office Buildings I torrioni di Vimodrone
Borgonovo, Milan, Italy

Parish Church
Attendorn, Germany, 2001–

Kindergarten
Rosà, Italy, 2001–

Private chapel, Azzano di Seravezza

Private Chapel
Azzano di Seravezza, Italy, 2001–02

Golf Club Hotel
Colle Val D'Elsa, Italy

BEIC European Library
Milan, Italy, competition

Belvedere Tower – Parco degli amici di Pinocchio
Collodi, Italy, 2001–

Office Building *Le Monarch*
Den Hague, The Netherlands, 2000–

Residences and Offices *Leipzigerplatz*
Berlin, Germany

Condominium Residences
Miami, Florida

Reconstruction and Extension of the Scala Theater
Milan, Italy, 2001–

Scala Theater, Milan

2002
Urban re-qualification of the ancient harbour area
Trieste, Italy

Masterplan for the re-qualification of the Falck area
Sesto San Giovanni, Milan, Italy

Residences
Prague, Czech Republic, competition

Reception Facilities and Hotel for the Faithful of Padre Pio
Pietrelcina, Italy, 2002–

Thalasso Therapy Center
Spotorno, Italy

Museum and Art Gallery of Tsinghua University
Beijing, China, 2002–

Tsinghua University, Beijing

Memorial 9/11 at the Pentagon
Washington DC, competition

Residences
Kilchberg, Switzerland, 2002

Auditorium and Multifunctional Pavilion
Bürgenstock, Switzerland

Residence and Office Tower
Pescara, Italy

Office, Residences and Hotel
Segrate, Italy

Redesign of Piazza Marconi and Embarcadero
Stresa, Italy

New Mariinsky Theater
St. Petersburg, Russia, competition

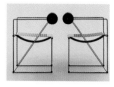

1982
Chair "Prima" (Alias)

Chair "Seconda" (Alias)

Longchair "Sesta" (Alias)

Lamp "Shogun" (Artemide)

1983
Table "Terzo" (Alias)

1984
Chair "Quarta" (Alias)

Exhibition "Carlo Scarpa 1906–1978",
Galleria dell'Accademia, Venice, Italy
(with Boris Podrecca)

Pitchers 1 (by Cleto Munari)

"Guscio" for the 17th Triennale of Milan, Italy

1986
Wall light "Fidia" (Artemide)

1985
Chair "Quinta" (Alias)

Door handles, FSB (Franz Schneider Brakel),
Brakel, Germany

Table "Tesi" (Alias)

Table lamp "Melanos" (Artemide)

Chair "Latonda" (Alias), 1987–88

Chair "Obliqua" (Alias), 1987–88

1989
Writing desk "Robot" (Alias)

Ceiling lamp "Zefiro" (Artemide)

Watch "Eye" (Alessi)

Pitchers 2 (by Cleto Munari)

1990
Carpets (Lantal Textiles)

Chair Botta 91 (Alias)

1992
Flower vase (by Cleto Munari)

Screen "Nilla Rosa" (Alias)

Set design for "Nutcracker", Opernhaus,
Zurich, Switzerland

1993
Set design for "Medea", Opernhaus,
Zurich, Switzerland

Exhibition Friedrich Dürrenmatt, Kunsthaus,
Zurich, Switzerland, 1993–94

1996
Pavilion for the Exhibition "Kolonihaven",
Copenhagen, Denmark, 1996–99

1994
Chair "Charlotte" (Strässle)

1997
Botta watch, 1997–98 (by Pierre Junod)

1998
Hanging Lamp "Mendrisio", 1996–98 (Artemide)
(with Dante Solcà)

Watch for the SFMOMA (Mondaine watch)

1995
Set design for "Ippolito", Stadttheater,
Basel, Switzerland

1999
Ceramic Flower Vase (8 from 13)

Urban furniture *Pausa* (by Benkert, Germany)

Pet and glass bottle design (for Valser Springs Ltd)

"Flower time" Clock (Mondaine watch), 1995–96

2000
Wine and water glass (for Cleto Munari)

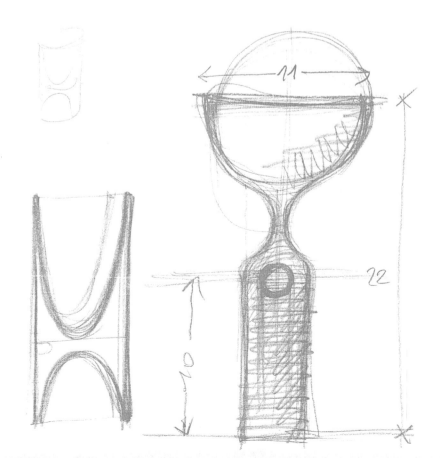